" ork
I admire and respect. She spreads her angelic wisdom with compassion and humility, and is one to watch on the spiritual scene."

Katy Evans, Editor of *Soul & Spirit*

"One of the most highly qualified 'angel teachers' I know, aring well-researched information and spiritual practices in holistic, loving and well-grounded way… [she] writes with a lovely easy style that is a pleasure to read."

William Bloom, author of *The Endorphin Effect* and *The Power of Modern Spirituality*

Chrissie has a genuine spiritual connection and shows great integrity in her work with the higher realms. Her amazing ngelic knowledge has brought angels into the lives of many thousands of people around the world."

Jacky Newcomb, *Sunday Times* best-selling author and paranormal experiences expert

Chrissie Astell is one of the most inspiring angel authorities writing at the present time. She wears her considerable erudition lightly and her teaching comes from the heart and from her direct experience of angels. Reading her books leaves one feeling uplifted, so a new one from her pen is always a delight."

vara d'Angelo, artist and author of *Angels in Our Time*

"Christine Astell is a true light worker in a very real sense. Her commitment to helping others reach angels, as she has, shines from every word she writes. Her words are capable of fanning the flames of belief, no matter how tiny the initial spark, in anyone who is troubled and seeking help. Some people have the gift to inspire joy, hope and serenity with every word, and the author is one of them."

Jenny Smedley, best-selling author of *Soul Angels*

"Chrissie Astell is one of the most authoritative speakers on angels that I know. Her knowledge of the angels and the gifts they bring us is brought out beautifully through her books, talks and seminars, but particularly in her meditations. It is so easy to connect with the angels with Chrissie's guidance and support and gentle encouragement."

Mairead Conlon, Spirit One Seminars (Dublin)

"It gives me real pleasure to say a few words about Chrissie Astell. I believe her to be one of the crystal children now emerging, a free-spirited, energetic teacher in the wisdom tradition of the Essenes, a leading light. She has marvellous energy and will accomplish all that she sets her heart upon, although most of us quail at the amount she undertakes. I wish her every success."

Anne MacEwen, co-founder and President of the Essene Network International

Dedicated to my mother, Sylvia Moss,
and to my father, Fred Astell, with a heart
full of love and gratitude to them both for
sharing the many blessed gifts of life with
me, in amazing and mysterious ways.

CONTENTS

FOREWORD

I have long been interested in worlds beyond the everyday one in which we work, relate to our friends and family and go about our daily routine. As a boy I experienced strange phenomena that convinced me there is a spirit world actively watching over our own – a world where those we have lost may be contacted, a world where forces of love and kindness are powerfully present. For me, angels are a part of this world. I experience them as a very real energy in my life.

Chrissie Astell's *Gifts from Angels* is the definitive book about angels. Chrissie shares with us her own personal experiences of interacting with angels as well as recounting wonderful stories from the many people she has met through her angel workshops and teaching. It is a beautifully written book that tells you everything you need to know about these amazing beings of light and how they manifest in our lives. Whether you believe in angels or not, this book is a joy to read. However downhearted or unhappy you are, *Gifts from Angels* will fill you with hope and the realization of just how much each one of us is loved.

I was moved to tears by some of the stories in this book. Chrissie's knowledge and expertise enables her to write about these glorious heavenly beings in a simple, easy-to-read way that is both fascinating and informative.

For myself I know that angels are real and that we are all capable of seeing or experiencing them. Reading this book will bring their loving energy closer to you.

William Roache, MBE
February 2011

INTRODUCTION

Angel Prayer

In the name of "I am that I am" I detach and let go of all energy in truth that is not mine.

I call back to myself all energy in truth that is mine and I ask that as it comes back to me it may be dissolved in the Love and the Light.

I call to the seven archangels and their Legions of Light.

I call to beloved Archangel Zadkiel and the Angels of Joy.

To Archangel Gabriel and the Angels of Wisdom,

to Archangel Michael and the Angels of Protection,

to Archangel Jophiel and the Angels of Illumination,

to Archangel Raphael and the Angels of Healing,

to Archangel Uriel and the Angels of Peace and

to Archangel Chamuel and the Angels of Love.

With gratitude in my heart I ask you to enter my earthly affairs and bring me your wonderful heavenly qualities.

Give me, please, the freedom from fear and self-doubt, that I may find in my mind your wisdom and illumination, understanding, inspiration, creativity, knowledge and clearness of sight.

Help me to fully appreciate and enjoy the qualities

of giving and receiving unconditional love; to feel compassion, mercy and forgiveness.

Show me how to dissolve the feelings of selfishness, self-condemnation and low self-esteem.

Give me the guidance I need to create inner peace and tranquillity in my heart and mind, and a truly spiritual balance in my humanness.

I ask that with the love and guidance of God, the source of all life, and with the help of the angels, I will grow to reach the understanding of true Christ consciousness.

As I ask, with honest intent, so may it be.

Amen

The word "angel", as we understand it, means "messenger". Angels are God's messengers, spiritual beings of light, acting as conduits between heaven and earth, carrying our prayers and petitions, hopes and fears, and returning on the instant with constant reassurance, guidance, healing and untold gifts of abundance in so many forms – if we choose to accept them.

Angels can appear in many different guises and, in their different forms, have always been a strong presence in the human imagination and spiritual experience. The law of "As above, so below" means that there is a hierarchy within the celestial ranks, similar to the hierarchies we have in our material world. The Seraphim and the Cherubim are the highest-ranking angels, who spend all their time and energy praising God and creating the flow of loving energy that is a fountain of God's pure loving light. This then flows down to archangels, who are closest to us.

The angels, among us in their multi-millions, are the messengers known as our guardians and protectors. The archangels are simply bigger energy forms: rather like generals or managers in charge of the heavenly hosts. They are capable of being in many places at any one time, and are part of the constantly changing universal form that we call "creation".

Angels in world religions

From the beginnings of recorded history there have been inspirational accounts of angelic visitations. We can read countless tales from all cultures, especially in books of scripture, in particular the Judaic and Christian

Bibles where angels appear many times, especially when something of importance is taking place. In Islam it is the angel Gabriel (Jibril) who is said to have dictated the Qur'an to Mohammed, while in the Mormon religion it was the angel Moroni who revealed to Joseph Smith the golden plates, from which the Book of Mormon was originally translated.

It was my fascination with this luminous thread of angelic presence that led me to study for myself the angels of every belief system, worldwide.

The inspiration of angels

There are many who can teach us, but one of my greatest inspirations has been St Teresa d'Avila. We can learn from the strength and tenacity of this diminutive woman, a divinely inspired sixteenth-century Carmelite nun. Her story is a remarkable account of trust and faith in the power of angels. At a time when others were being sought out and executed by the Spanish Inquisition, when women were not allowed to teach and Jews were being persecuted for their faith (her grandfather was a Jew), and when writing in the vernacular was forbidden (only Latin and Greek were allowed), it was she who wrote books about spirituality and the angels and taught prayers in Spanish to her novices. Despite all odds, St Theresa miraculously avoided persecution and went on to reform the monastic system throughout Spain, founding the Discalced ("shoeless") order.

William Blake, the great artist and mystic, is renowned for his accounts of angelic visitations. There is a marvellous story of how his mother sent him off to paint an angel, and as he called out, "How am I supposed to paint an angel when I have never seen one?" a voice is reputed to have answered, "I will sit for you, I am Gabriel."

A little later in the eighteenth century, the scientist-turned-mystic Swedenborg had experiences of being taken to heaven by angels. There he was shown how angels evolve and was left with the knowledge that we, as human beings, are all capable of becoming "angels" or messengers of God. After his experiences he wrote that it was likely his peers would disbelieve him, but that nothing would ever take away what he had seen and what he now knew.

Then there are real-life stories from throughout the modern world wars of angel sightings. Soldiers of the World War I reported seeing glowing men on horseback galloping through the sky toward enemy lines. Many men returning from the World War II told of being guided through mine fields and of mysterious nurses who tended their wounds before disappearing.

Angel stories

This is a book of angel stories – all first-hand accounts of experiences with angels – and there is much that we can learn from them. Perhaps they jog a half-forgotten memory of a similar, unexplained occurrence in our own life or maybe they give us "Ah-ha" moments of deep recognition and understanding.

There is nothing new about these stories, except to say that they have not been written down before. Many of my own encounters with angels, the awesome ministry of celestial helpers, are told here for the first time. If you have been to one of my workshops, then I may have told you some of my stories in person, but I hope that you will enjoy being reminded of their magic and beauty.

Angels are found throughout history guiding, protecting and healing, just as they do today. The angelic world is not bound by time: may the timeless gifts from angels continue to bless you, your life and that of your loved ones, for ever.

The aim of this book

In this book I shall be passing on various "gift" experiences of divine intervention and illustrating the strength of each one by relating some real-life stories told by friends, my workshop and course participants and my readers. I will also be sharing some of the stories of colleagues and friends who have dedicated their lives to spiritual teaching or angel work, showing how an angelic experience can lead to an important change of life direction. All the people who sent me their stories to share with you believe that the angels stepped in to help, save, guide, protect or simply leave a sign of divine presence – and they all believe that this help is available to us all.

The chapters

Each chapter in this book brings you stories about how people have been helped by angels in their lives. Each ends with an affirmation and guided visualization, so that you, too, can participate and enjoy the gifts the angels bring to share.

Chapter 1, Gifts of Love, tells of the different ways

we, as human beings, can experience the measureless, unconditional love of God through the angels.

Chapter 2, Gifts of Protection, relates how angels protect us physically, emotionally and spiritually in the most unexpected ways.

Chapter 3, Gifts of Healing, illustrates how angelic energy can heal all aspects of our lives, including our relationships and finances, as well as our mind, body and soul.

Chapter 4, Gifts of Guidance and Wisdom, describes how guidance may come through different methods: whispered voices, strange lights and chance encounters.

Chapter 5, Gifts of Creativity, explains how we are all co-creators of our universe. In our small, individual worlds it is not always possible to see the bigger picture as the angels see it, so this chapter will help such insight.

Chapter 6, Gifts of Courage, will inspire you to take heart, at any stage of your life.

Chapter 7, Gifts of Peace, shows that it is through inner peace that we will find the way, whether we seek peace close to home, perhaps in family relationships, or globally, in terms of world peace.

Angels in our lives

Over the past twelve years of travelling and conducting workshops, it has become my living affirmation that I meet wonderful people who have angels in their lives. Many of them, like me, have changed their lives because they have encountered angels. After all, we have something in common: a belief, perhaps, that we have been called to work with the angels here on earth – to try to make a difference. So many people, worldwide, are re-awakening to the gentle rhythm of their own spiritual impulse. I wonder, do we *all* have something in common? Do we attract one another because we are part of the same universal driving force? Are we truly all *One*? And, could it be true that we share an intimate understanding, personal and profound, that unfolds gradually, deep in the core of our soul, when we remember that we have been called to work in service with the angels here on earth?

Making connection

Gradually, as each of us wakens to that angel clarion call as single bright sparks of light, we recognize one another and make connection, like electrical impulses joining forces. When all our small bright lights are shining together, we ignite a powerful cosmic flame; a passionate force for good that really makes a difference in the world. The difference to what and to whom becomes clearer as our journey into the spiritual life progresses. Leading a more spiritual life certainly does not mean that everything becomes easier, or the journey smoother. But the way we perceive the challenges along the way does seem to change radically.

Minor shifts and major change

Sometimes we make minor shifts, which affect how we acknowledge and nurture our spiritual self and others. This may even become the catalyst for a total life change. Is this major life change the point at which angels come into our lives bearing gifts? Is this what guides and inspires us, connecting with our heart in such a way that we can rediscover our true soul purpose? The answer is very likely yes, but not always. When you read some of the stories that follow you will see that angels step in at times of distress, but also that they enable us to help other people in enchanting ways that would perhaps go unnoticed by those with half-closed eyes.

Spiritual fruits

Even in our modern society, where being "religious" is often seen as negative, and the suggestion of it used as a put-down, there is always a way for the light of the soul to shine. My view is that we are spiritual beings of light enjoying a human experience rather than human beings trying to find our soul.

I once saw a fridge magnet that read, "God wants spiritual fruits, not religious nuts". It brought back memories of my first husband's constant threat that if I wasn't careful I would become a religious nutcase, like my parents. The magnet made me smile and, just like my quest for a more spiritual existence, the phrase stayed with me. I memorized and later borrowed it to use as a teaching point in my *Advice from Angels* book and cards, as I thought it highly relevant to our time.

Fanaticism and dogma are not enlightening. Is it not better to sow gently the seeds of wisdom and love, allowing them to develop and mature in their own time? There is nothing spiritual or enlightening in imposing one's beliefs on others. All the great master-teachers taught in simple parables, which were easily accessible to all levels of understanding. How inspiring and motivating to be able to share with those who are reaping the harvest of their own spiritual growth.

Why this book is for you

If you are reading this book, then you are surely already interested in angels. Perhaps you are conversant with them and are already working as a healer or teacher, assisting others in finding their angelic connection. Or perhaps you have had an experience that you find hard to explain and are seeking answers. Or maybe you have not had an angel experience but enjoy reading about the experiences of others. Or perhaps you are slightly sceptical and are reading this book so that you can arrive at your own conclusions.

Whatever your attraction to angels, it is likely that you are being called. The angel clarion call is heard far and wide, by any of our senses. You do not have to be religious, highly sensitive or conversant with the esoteric – angels appear to ordinary people in very extraordinary circumstances, and to extraordinary people in very ordinary, day-to-day circumstances. This is your opportunity to share some of the many true stories in which angels have brought gifts from the Divine in one form or another.

A loving presence

Those of us who have been in the presence of an angel can never forget the experience. It leaves behind a deeply embodied connection, which can never be taken away. Whether a life has been saved or a profound truth discovered, each recipient is left with the knowledge that he or she will never again be alone. The sensation described by many is that of a loving presence so vivid and strong that they were truly overwhelmed. Some people, having been touched by the presence of an angel, become healers; some simply change their lifestyle or become stronger in their faith and more confident in their connection to the Divine.

My hope for you

However these stories of true, angelic connection leave you feeling, my hope, in sharing them with you, is that if the spark of divine love in your own soul has dimmed, then it will be re-ignited. If you have ever felt alone or troubled, reading about the experiences of others may remind you of serendipitous occasions in your own life when the angels have perhaps been present.

Effects of angel work

I feel that angelic presence has had an extraordinary effect on my life, as it can on yours, too. In my work I meet people who share a connection with their spiritual energies and I have made scores of good friendships. I have developed a role that serves others, at the same time deepening my own sense of angelic and psychic connection. As I learn to strengthen my own spiritual practices I'm also helping others to discover their own. Without angelic guidance I would not be doing this.

How I made my angel connection

You could say my mid-life career change was inevitable. Throughout my twenties and thirties, when I was bringing up two children and running a family business, I knew inside that there was something else I was meant to be doing. I sought guidance through psychics, mediums, tarot readers, healers, astrologers and the Christian church, but no one knew what it was I was supposed to be doing in my life. Teacher, healer, writer, spiritual mentor, counsellor all seemed options, but no one could tell me how to find and follow my path. My father gently insisted that everything would fall into place when the time was right – when God knew I was ready.

It was following a painful separation in 1997 that I took up the career that would lead me along an irreversible spiritual journey. I was desperate to leave a business that made me so miserable I became ill, and I returned to my old nursing career through a series of divine coincidences, which I now know to have been guided by the angels. Somehow, I was always in the right place at the right time to make the connections.

I met an "angel teacher", who brought out my teaching and healing abilities and asked me to co-host angel workshops with her. In my enthusiasm I flew to Los Angeles (the "city of angels") and met people who sold beautiful angel artefacts for the home. I became convinced that I should open a shop selling similar merchandise, with healing rooms to nurture the mind, body and soul. But in a vivid dream I was shown that this was not the right place, time or role for me.

The beginning of my angel work

It was while I was nursing in a residential home, and working in a hospice on my days off, that my angel work really started in earnest. I loved my work and was happy to have returned to my original career of nursing. My children had lives of their own by now and being single again was a blessing. But it was while I was on nursing duty that my life took another turn. A patient fell and, in my rush to help him, I badly hurt my back. My sick leave gave me the opportunity to reassess my work life and make the decision to devote my entire career to spiritual teaching.

I obtained a degree in comparative religion, then went on to gain post-graduate certificates in spiritual development and facilitation, and teaching in lifelong learning. Those four years were hectic. Most of my spare time was taken up with "angel parties": evening talks and sessions in people's houses, introducing angels and guided meditation and selling angel books and gifts.

I lived on the top floor of a large factory conversion, with hundreds of apartments, and my car was kept down in the basement. Every morning, as I waited for the garage doors to rise, I would call each of the seven archangels to be with me and bestow their gifts of blessing on me in every aspect of my day. This ritual soon developed into a prayer that I would repeat every time I left the building. By the time I reached the road I would be glowing and calm.

Gradually, angels became a more and more important part of my spiritual life. I would call upon Michael for protection, Gabriel for wisdom and guidance, Chamuel for love and self-esteem, Zadkiel for joy, Jophiel for enlightenment, Uriel for strength and peace and Raphael for healing.

Angel messages

It is important to pay attention to what angels are telling us. To tune in to angel energy, to meet, see, sense or feel the angels, to work in service alongside them and to love and appreciate what they do for us is as much, or more than, any expectation the angelic realms would have of us. The urgent message coming from the angels during our present time of great change is one of interconnectedness. Their hope is that, by sharing their gifts, we will remember our connection, our role as preservers of nature, our responsibility as custodians of this beautiful planet – our home – while we experience our soul's journey through time.

Unexpected gifts

As we progress on life's journey, many of us will quite naturally be drawn closer to, or further away from, our spiritual centre, depending on our choices and interpretations of our life experiences. Looking back over my own life, I can see that it was mostly on the occasions when I wasn't nurturing the spiritual aspects that I was helped the most. This is probably true for most people. For me, these experiences were divine gifts from God and the angels, given because I am, like all of us, so loved.

As children of God we are constantly plied with a variety of gifts of opportunity. Life is an abundant source of synchronicities, coincidences, chance encounters, much-loved objects mysteriously recovered when lost, strangers appearing from nowhere just when we need them, super-human strength in crises, fleeting fragrances, whispers and feathers. Are all these simply part of normal human experience or could they be gifts from the angels?

The greatest gift

Of all the many gifts offered us, the gift of love is the greatest gift of all and one that can be experienced by each of us in many ways. However, it is a gift that, without consciously meaning to, we can reject over and over again, although it is the one emotion we consistently seek. Ask any group of people what they most desire in a human relationship, above all else, and the majority will tell you that they just want to feel loved. Many of us search throughout life for love, feeling that it permanently evades us. Some people feel they need to earn it, mistaking their need for love as a need of approval. Some have low self-esteem and, feeling unloved, fail to recognize loving gestures they are already experiencing, while others are so cocooned by smother-love that they take love for granted.

The Essene Network

One of my most profound experiences of love involves a group of people known as the Essenes. The modern Essene Network, to which I belong, was formed to re-establish a closer cooperation with the angels in accordance with the teachings discovered in the Dead Sea Scrolls. Historically, the Essenes were a Jewish sect, living on the shores of the Dead Sea, who understood the cosmic powers of nature and structured their lives accordingly. They called the *energy forces of nature*

"Angels of the Earthly Mother", and the *universal cosmic forces* "Angels of the Heavenly Father". They held to daily meditations and angel communions as a regular spiritual practice and adhered to a diet of raw, natural foods.

This gave them a deep understanding of the balance between the spiritual and physical aspects of life. By pursuing a life of healthy devotion to food of the body, mind and spirit, many of the Essenes became healers and teachers in the community. Belonging to this sect were John the Baptist and the great Essene teacher, Master Jesus. They understood the need for harmony within and with all of nature, and their way of life is just as applicable today as it was over two thousand years ago. It is believed that many healers among us today are Essenes returned to assist in the "re-awakening" of spiritual consciousness and to help us to return to a life of compassion and love.

Questions about angels

Will working with the angels and inviting them into our daily life automatically heighten our ability to love and be loved? Or, do we attract angels to come closer to us because of the loving nature of our soul? Are the seemingly loveless personal hardships and challenges we encounter on our journey simply a result of our choosing a difficult, or even wrong, route?

These are some of the many questions I often ask myself as I tiptoe along my own spiritual pathway, and especially when I struggle with the balance between a "normal" family life and my chosen spiritual path. Some people believe that there is no such thing as the "wrong" decision, or the "wrong" path, only varying degrees of ease or difficulty.

There are so many things to consider. Is it true that we are living out our own karma of cause and effect from previous lifetimes, and that our experiences are meant to help us develop empathy with others and deepen our compassionate nature?

Are we called to work with the angelic realms because we are naturally loving, compassionate and kind? Or, if God is Love, and the angels are fashioned as aspects of God's divine nature, are we called because doing heaven's work with the grace of the angels' presence proves to strengthen and nurture love, compassion and kindness within us?

Are we chosen on merit or, as I believe, have we already agreed to be of service before we are incarnated into this life? And since we normally "forget" our soul's purpose the moment we are born, are these angelic interventions a push in the direction we were originally meant to be taking, serving to remind us of who we really are?

Encounters with angels

Angel encounters are varied and widely experienced. As we read the stories in this book, we may think we can clearly see the angels' gift, that it is obvious. But we are only the onlookers. We will never really know what the individual lesson was, or even if it was ever learned. The real essence of the gift is always a secret between giver and receiver.

I have received many stories from my workshop participants and from readers of my website all over the world. The majority of angel gifts seem to be for the purpose of protection, empowerment, safety and strength. I have personally experienced these gifts many times, even when I had no idea what they meant.

One of the most commonly asked questions people have is "When did it all start – when did you first start believing in angels?" This is difficult to answer. The angels seem to have drifted in and out of my life, but I can't think of a time when I did not believe in them. Looking back with amusement and embarrassment at some of the scrapes my younger self experienced, I know that I always had a guardian angel by my side.

My early life

My background and upbringing have meant that a spiritual path of some sort would always be my destiny. I was a very sensitive child and I also had a vivid imagination. When I was small I saw ribbons of light circling my room. Faces would appear and sometimes I heard laughter, too. A sceptic might suggest that this was something to do with car headlights and childish fantasies… perhaps, but perhaps not!

My young parents married, had me, but then separated. My father left when I was two to follow, through a series of bizarre coincidences, a strange and mystical path. He joined Peter and Eileen Caddy, who later, following divine guidance, founded the Findhorn community in Scotland. My mother, torn apart by what was front-page scandal at that time, was forced to move house. She decided to become a nurse and I went to live with my grandmother.

My grandparents' influence

Abandonment issues aside, I was very fortunate spiritually. My grandma believed in fairies and taught me to sit quietly at the bottom of the garden among the marigolds, where I might hear the music of fairy bells ringing, if I was lucky. Any doubt from me brought a response of, "If there are no fairies, who hangs the dew drops on the spider's web, and who rings the bluebells in the spring?"

A firm believer in an afterlife and guardian angels, she also taught me that we are never alone. We shared tales of the supernatural as well as cuddles, buns and sweet tea. There were also Christian stories passed on by my great-grandfather, a Methodist preacher, and I certainly knew of Mrs "Doasyouwouldbedoneby" from the Victorian moral tale of *The Water Babies*, which my granddad read to me.

My grandma loved Celtic folk tales, was very psychic and often talked of her previous lives. She taught me to bake pastry, darn socks, embroider, read the tea leaves and to trust my intuition. So, my spiritual and creative self was allowed to blossom and flourish. We lived on the coast and, being free-spirited, I wandered and played, sometimes for the whole day. I never really felt lonely, even though I longed for a home with a "normal" mummy and daddy like my friends at school. However, it was as though there was always someone there with me. I was always catching a glimpse of someone or something out of the corner of my eye. Regardless of whether my grandma knew where I was, or what I was up to, I always felt that someone was looking after me.

My early religious education

I have felt the protection of a divine presence many times in my life. As I grew up I was confident in strong religious beliefs, without any intellectual understanding of defined religion. I talked to God in simple prayer and conversation. Like many children in the fifties and sixties I went to Sunday school, regardless of whether or not my parents attended church. Clearly there was a strong family connection with the church through my great-grandfather's influence, and it was thought that regular church attendance would "do me good" and "keep me on the right track". Of course it may have had that effect, to a degree, but my own suspicion is that my attendance at Sunday school was to give my poor grandma a break from my lively antics for a couple of hours.

My special friend

Even though I was afraid of the dark as a child, I loved the thrill of walking home through dark side streets. I felt exhilarated and brave to be skipping along through the winter darkness because I had a friend with me. My friend stopped anyone from leaping out of dark shop doorways. My friend saved me from the shadows of rustling shrubberies and protected me as I crossed the busy roads. My friend was always with me. I sang songs to him learnt at Sunday school. His name was Jesus, and my grandma told me he loved all children. She often told me that Jesus was the friend of every child, because it says in the Bible that He suffered the little children to come to Him. Of course I didn't understand fully, but when I was irritating my grandma, she sometimes called me "insufferable". In my little head, I worked out there must be a connection in her choice of word that meant Jesus loved me, too.

Following in my parents' footsteps

My mother actually saw fairy folk as a child and has communicated with the beings that some call ascended masters, as well as with the angels, for about fifty years. She moved to Oregon, USA, in the seventies, to build an eco-community called Alcyone, a centre for spiritual enlightenment near Mount Shasta. She has told me many stories of the spiritual gatherings held there at the "dawning of the New Age". Combine my mother's interests with those of my spiritual healer father, a modern Christian mystic and spiritual mentor, and there seemed little doubt that one day I, too, would be following a spiritual path of service. It has fascinated me that both my parents have led such intensely spiritual lives, though neither brought me up, and at times they had very little to do with me. Deeper understanding has shown me how to embrace the "bigger picture", knowing that all is exactly as it is meant to be.

Prophecy and fulfilment

Once married, my then husband would have no part in my spiritual quest and little truck with those he thought relied on religion as a "crutch". Harsh words, which hurt. He said that if I didn't take care I, too, would become "religious", and possibly end up running away from real-life responsibilities, just like my own parents had done. Of course these prophecies were partly true.

But what comes first – prophecy or fulfilment? Energy follows thought, after all. In my case it was inevitable; I did eventually move away, and I did end up following a spiritual life, which became my work and my journey. It was simply "in the genes".

Early adult life

I left home in the north of England when I was seventeen and hit the bright lights to work in the travel industry, before becoming a nurse. I was seeking "something". I felt I had a purpose, a job I had to do, a mission and I tried several careers. It was the transport industry, later on, that almost killed me!

After we married, my husband decided to leave the Metropolitan Police to run his own business and an opportunity came for him to buy an overnight parcel-delivery franchise. My instinct told me this was wrong for us; I did not want to go ahead and was fearful. Nevertheless it was what he wanted to do and the stress of resisting became intolerable.

With two small children in tow I became a white-van driver, a sales representative, an employer, a parcel packer and a miserable wife and mother. We worked from the early hours until midnight every day and our marriage broke down. We had two lovely children, but the business completely eroded our family life. Depression hit me hard, and by the time I was planning my own suicide it was obvious that I needed help.

I had blocked out the angels and I can see now that I had allowed my spiritual self to be crushed. This was a disaster in terms of my holistic health. I now understand that, if we don't nurture our spirit, we can become terribly disturbed.

My spiritual quest

I secretly joined a confirmation class at my local church but this didn't provide me with the kind of guidance or comfort I was seeking. At times of despair I could not imagine being more unhappy. Even though I had no self-esteem and felt totally worthless, whenever I was desolate gentle voices whispered in my head, "Christine, it doesn't have to be like this."

After yet another row with my husband I broke down; sobbing until breathless I called to God to either take me or help me. In an instant I was calm and my breathing had become normal. I stood up, with an inner strength I had never felt before. Running through every cell of my body was a sense of knowing that everything was going to be fine.

A turning point

Divine help came in the form of a family counsellor. My husband had suggested marriage guidance, but ultimately didn't come along himself. What a gift this turned out to be for me.

The counsellor, also called Christine, practised Aura Soma therapy and took a holistic approach to marriage guidance. In her consulting room she kept an array of pretty, coloured bottles and these intrigued me. One of them, in shades of pale blue and pink, caught my attention and every week I was drawn to its gorgeous colours. One day I finally asked what the bottles were for, and told her that I was very drawn to one in particular. Christine explained that this was my soul bottle. The blue and pink mixture of flower essence and oils was called "Orion and Angelica" and represented the two angel guardians of the curtains at the heavenly gates. I was told they had escorted my soul as I came to the earth plane. The angels had brought me here and I was to work closely with them.

How bizarre, I thought. If I am here to work with angels, why don't I already know it? And, if it were true, surely I would be having a better life than this!

Possibility of change

From that moment, I began to find safe places to talk to angels; usually when I was sitting by trees or near a local pond. I asked them to help me sort out my life. I told them that if they wanted my help I was willing, but they would have to give me courage to make changes. I then attended a "healing with angels" course, and there found all the courage I needed.

My life certainly changed. I refer flippantly to the day when I became "young, free and single" again, but change often comes at a price, sometimes a painful one. My husband agreed to move out, but then reneged and I had to leave everything behind, including my teenage children. I moved into a flat on my own, to save my sanity. My children were old enough to make choices, too. My son was already working, but my daughter refused to move with me. Leaving her family home and all her close friends was too difficult.

New lives

Gradually we all found happier lives. We were all blessed and cared for throughout the challenges that came along. My son travelled the world as a chef and my daughter fell in love with a gentle young man, whom she later married. My ex-husband eventually changed his life dramatically and is now in a happy relationship, too.

I loved my little flat and I found a job. Miraculously, with synchronicity, everything fell into place. Every time I prayed for help with the next obstacle, I received instant divine intervention from the angels in the form of "coincidences". I was hugely grateful and decided to help others find their angels and a way to a joyful life. I enjoyed my job as a nurse and running angel workshops in any spare time. My life was challenging, yet satisfying. During this transition I felt very close to the angelic realms. Day after day mini-miracles took place and the staff and residents sometimes said they could feel a difference on the unit when I was on duty. The angelic presence I seemed to bring with me was tangible.

CHAPTER 1

GIFTS OF LOVE

The angels are among us to show us that only love matters, above all else. Yet so many of us remain closed to love. Experiences of pain and emotional trauma can mean that we find it difficult to love ourselves, and we may feel even less able to love others without placing conditions upon them. This makes it harder for us to open our heart to the love of others. The Archangel Chamuel and the Angels of Love bear the gift of unconditional and unlimited love to share with us. Here are some experiences of how that love feels.

And now abideth faith, hope, love, these three;
and the greatest of these is love.

I CORINTHIANS 13:13

Love – the greatest gift of all. Faith is felt as trust and as the anchor of the soul by many, while hope is an anticipation yet to be fulfilled, but love of all the eternal virtues is the greatest, because love alone is divine. It is an elusive gift we so often crave, but sometimes fail to recognize. We count on love in the form of affection from others, but if we take love for granted, it may be a prize that we carelessly destroy. In our busy world we sometimes crave for a more peaceful life, but without love the peace is empty. If we choose, we can find many things to occupy our time and live a full and busy life, but without love it is all just tiring and meaningless. Love, or at least the romantic, human kind, which the poets call "Eros" can seem elusive, intangible and evasive. It has been the object of dreams, art, music, poetry and prose since the beginning of time.

Angelic love

And yet we do have love. We are all loved. In fact we are so loved and cherished that we have been given the priceless gift of angels. Each and every one of us has an angel that guides, guards, encourages, empowers, heals, protects and loves us completely. Angelic love is pure. It is a state of being where there are no conditions, no excuses, and no lack of commitment. This kind of love will never count cost, never take back, never abandon, never be jealous or controlling, resentful or irritable. Best of all, it will never turn us away. All we have to do is open our heart and choose to accept it.

We all experience emotions, whatever they may mean to us subjectively. It is often too hard to understand,

and even harder to empathize with, the experiences of another person if we have not been in a similar position. And so, for a subject as personal and close to the heart as love itself, I am starting with stories and examples from my own experience, as these are easier for me to describe with authenticity.

My visitation story

First, let me share with you my own angel visitation story, when I experienced angelic love – a truly celestial gift. The day I saw an angel left me with no doubt that pure, heavenly, unconditional love exists, and the role I would play in sharing that message became crystal clear to me.

My angelic visitation happened one afternoon as I was sitting in my little flat after I had finished my shift at the nursing home. I remember clearly how much I was enjoying one of my angel books – a recommended one written by Eileen Elias Freeman, who had been a church minister in America and had created her own liturgies to the angels.

The piece I was reading was particularly suitable for my angel groups and workshops. I read it twice and I was suddenly overwhelmed with emotion as I read the words aloud, invoking the archangels Raphael, Uriel, Michael and Gabriel in a ritual for healing the earth. As tears ran softly down my face I called out in frustration to the heavens, "I have dedicated the rest of my life in service to you. Oh why can I not see you? Please angels, who are you? Show yourself. Please, let me see you."

A dazzling vision

I was staring up toward the sky, as I so often do. And as I looked out the window, instantly there was a dazzling bright light in front of me, shining through the glass. It seemed to illuminate the whole room and I stood up and walked to the window. There in front of me, as clear as day in the sky, was a huge white angel.

I stared. I could hardly believe my eyes as the light became even brighter. I wanted to see the face and yearned to recognize it, as I so often see faces in my meditations, particularly when I'm giving healing. But instead of having features, the face was made of the brightest golden light, as bright as the sun, and I couldn't even look at it.

I was surprised to sense a strong masculine presence and was amazed to see two pairs of wings. One huge pair reached high, pointing up into the sky, like the elegant stroke of a paintbrush. The other pair was more curved and folded behind the angel's back. I stared at the beautiful feet and toes. I could almost feel the silk fabric of the gown, which swayed gently in the air. Then, as I stood and connected with this beautiful, magnificent, majestic being, I absolutely knew in my heart that I recognized him and that this angel absolutely knew me, too. And not only that he knew me – I knew that he loved me.

Pure love

I had not experienced that feeling of love before or since; it can't even be adequately described. I have never found the right words and I guess that this is what the mystics call "the ineffable". Every cell in my body, mind and soul felt totally, blissfully loved, and in love. All I could do was stand and stare, with tears pouring down my cheeks – tears not of sadness, but of pure joy and recognition. I knew him… I really knew him!

The angel held out his hands to me. Both arms moved together in a gesture of giving and receiving. His hair was white and shoulder-length and it moved; his robe moved and his hands moved, too. He was absolutely real. It was almost as if, in that moment, that split second, if I had chosen to, I could have left my body and flown into his arms. Then the angel turned on to his side and drifted away into the sky. I thought my heart would stop and I wanted to call out for him to take me with him. But I remembered that we have to be careful what we wish for – and anyway I had work to do. All I could do was stand and watch.

A few seconds later, a large cerise-coloured heart appeared in the sky where the angel had been. It was just as if someone had drawn it there. It was breathtakingly beautiful: so precise, so perfect, so pink! What did it mean? Was that a gift of love for me? Was it the angel's way of saying "I love you"? Or, was he telling me that I was supposed to share my heart with others?

As I watched, I panicked. I didn't want to fail my beautiful celestial messenger in my ignorance. I heard no voice, no words of instruction, no wonderful music, no loud trumpets. I suddenly felt terribly inadequate and I chastised myself for not knowing what to do. Then it came to me like a warm glow. I knew that the heart was the angel's name. He was "Love" and I was working with the angels from the realms of love. The angel was showing me that only love really matters. Nothing else. Universal, divine love was the message I was destined to share.

I immediately phoned my father, a close spiritual friend and mentor by now. "I've just seen an angel," I blurted out as he picked up the phone. "Have you, darling?" came the gentle response. "And what did it look like?" I described every detail. "Yes," he said, "I believe you have. You must work hard, dear. This message has been given to me, too, by the angels, and you must pass it on to as many people as you can. That is your job now."

There is a Zen Buddhist saying, "You cannot tread the Path before you become the Path yourself." I needed to "feel" that experience before I could truly understand what the gift of God's love really was. Without the message from my angel visitation would I have ever felt the intensity of love that I have craved so many times in this life? Would I have ever been able to empathize and connect with others who have felt it too?

Dan's story

Sometimes the angels bring deeply personal messages that we are unable to share, so they remain a secret, held within our heart for ever. At other times they bring a message of love for us to pass on to others. Even when the message is for someone else, the angels' presence fills us with an indescribable sensation of personal bliss. This phenomenon is expressed by Dan in the following story. Dan is a keen master practitioner of NLP (Neuro-Linguistic Programming), a Reiki master and one of my long-standing students. He gave me this message:

I felt very connected to the energies of Archangel Gabriel. So I was meditating and listening to my MP3 player on my way to work: it was the beautiful music accompanying your visualization meditation with the Archangel Jophiel, for light and creativity. As I finished the visualization, sitting on the train with plenty of time, I switched off my MP3 player and relaxed with my eyes closed, enjoying the sensations that the meditation had brought to me. Suddenly, I became aware of an overwhelming brightness. It not only completely engulfed me and where I was sitting, but seemed to be lighting up the whole carriage. As I opened my eyes there was a vibrant light shining all around me. I wondered if anyone else could see this, too, but judging by the blank expressions in the morning rush hour, there was no evidence of this.

I knew that I was in the presence of angels. There was white light to one side and bright golden light to the other. I believed the light to be the essence of the Archangel Jophiel, with whom I had just been communing. I was filled with awe at such beauty and overwhelmed by the love flowing through me; it was amazing and I knew everything was good. But then I realized that the feeling I had was of two angels, and I had an inner knowing that the presence of Gabriel was with me, too. I became aware that they were communicating with me and then I heard a message for you, Chrissie, "Let it be, just let it be. All will be well."

One fascinating aspect of Dan's message was the timing. I had been feeling particularly frustrated by interrelated issues, which I had been trying to resolve all at once. Even though I had been asking for, and trusting in, angelic assistance, human nature had got in the way.

When we allow emotional attachment to block our spiritual connections, the angels may use other, clearer channels to get their message through.

"I knew I was given that message for you," Dan puzzled. "It definitely wasn't meant for me, and yet I was left completely filled with love. What an amazing side-effect of being useful!"

Karen's story

Karen, a complementary therapist, decided to share her angel encounter with me. Training to be a crystal therapist, she had finished her first year and had a year to go. She was doing a lot of meditation and realizes now that she was opening up to different energies.

I was standing in my downstairs bathroom, idly looking at the wall. The wall was plain white at the time and I had been wondering about putting something inspirational on it. I was thinking of painting on a verse with a huge rainbow around it. Anyway I was just looking at the wall, trying to envision what to put there, when I noticed that high up in the right-hand corner there was a slight pinkish colour. As I kept looking, the pinkish "mist" began to move and spread across the wall. This pink colour also encompassed reds and a sort of purplish blue. Then it all started swirling around and a huge heart shape began to form in the middle.

I closed my eyes at one point to double-check whether what I was seeing was real or not. When connecting to other energies I often get a feeling of a bright light being shone in my eyes, although my eyes are closed, and sure enough when I closed my eyes the light was very bright indeed. I opened them and the colour faded to a light pink, but was still there across the top half of the wall.

I have angel cards, so I took them out and asked for clearer guidance and also to know which angel had visited me. The two cards that came out of the deck were "Fun" and Archangel Chamuel, who is on the pink ray and deals with love. I burst into tears at this point. I could feel the energy and the message meant so much to me. Even a few days later I could feel the presence of this angel near to me.

Everybody I had met at work earlier that day had been wearing bright pink. I remember commenting on my friend's pink shoes and saying how lovely they were.

Karen has no doubt that Archangel Chamuel came to visit and to give her the message she needed to hear at that time. She is working toward running her own business in crystal healing and giving people the message that love can change anything and that we can change ourselves from within at any time.

Kay's story

The angels understand how hard we human beings struggle to find true love. They try to engineer situations for our lessons to be learned, but sadly we are often our own worst enemies. We miss the messages and often fail to learn from our mistakes along the way, creating patterns of behaviour that lead to more difficult situations and challenges. Here are two stories about human love. The first is from Kay, one of my students, who shares her story of romantic love.

The angels have brought me much wisdom and many blessings throughout my life, but I cannot think of a more beautiful gift than to have led me to my soulmate John. It was nearing the end of 2009 and I was feeling really down because I hadn't found a man to share my life with. There I was, fifty-eight years old, with two failed marriages behind me and two live-in relationships that had not worked either. It didn't usually get to me this much, but I had just said goodbye to another male friend and I had almost given up on finding my soulmate.

That evening a strange but reassuring event took place as I had my daily conversation with God. It was late and I was in bed. In the darkness, I poured my heart out to Him, saying that I felt I deserved a good man in my life – after all I had devoted much of my life to helping others find happiness and peace of mind; surely it was my turn. Not the usual way to speak to God. However, that is how I felt. As I opened my eyes, I saw a shaft of very bright blue light directly in front of me, at the end of the bed. Was this a sign that Archangel Michael was with me? I felt very calm and peaceful, even joyful. Somewhere deep inside I knew that this would herald a change in my romantic circumstances. I didn't understand how or when, but I sensed that 2010 would be the year when I would meet the man I would want to spend the rest of my life with.

Just before Christmas, Aiden, husband of my dear sister, Jan, gave me an email address of a work colleague. His name was John. Aiden said that he had a good feeling about John and we would have lots in common, but that I should take care because his wife had died about a year before. It was clear that Aiden liked John and wanted to help me in my quest for love. However I didn't manage to contact John over Christmas, and didn't give him much thought.

In the New Year, I joined Chrissie's spiritual study group and discovered her unique guided visualizations with the archangels. They prompted me to ask again for blessings from God and the angels, to bring love into my life. Out of the blue, I heard from John in January, via a message on Facebook. He told me about himself and how he missed his departed wife and how sad he was. We continued to write for a couple of months and, eventually, he asked me to meet him when I next came to visit Jan and Aiden. We all met over dinner in a pub and it was a nice evening as the four of us had plenty to talk about.

John turned out to be lovely but a little distant, which I could understand because his wife had died only fifteen months earlier. Initially I didn't think anything would come of it, but John and I arranged to meet at Easter and spent the day and evening together. We talked for hours about our lives and aspirations, our beliefs and dreams, and came to the conclusion that we were compatible. We even spoke about how we felt about marriage. It was a fantastic day and I couldn't wait to see him again.

After that the romance blossomed effortlessly. We spent almost every weekend together, and by October had decided to take a leap of faith and move into a little cottage together. Our lives have changed in such an exciting and dramatic way and I know that my lovely sister and her husband put that change into motion when they introduced us. But I'm convinced that the archangels had a strong influence on the process, too. It was their guiding light that gave me the confidence to start a new friendship at a time when I was at my lowest. And my guardian angel's presence has been with me in my weekly meditations, gently encouraging me to trust my instincts in seeking love. I know that without that heavenly guidance I would probably not have found such a wonderful partner – the greatest gift I could have wished for.

David's story

The second story of love is from David. He is one of my regular students, who has been enjoying his connection with angels for several years. He told me a wonderful story of how the angels had shown him how to "let go" and really love himself. As one of my more enthusiastic students, David worked very hard on the exercises and practices I suggested and was developing a real sense of joy in his work as a schoolteacher.

I am so happy in my work and the daily meditations help to create a real presence around me, which I know is lifting me into a state of pure joy. I have never been confrontational, but now I feel I have evolved somehow (spiritually); everyone keeps telling me how the staffroom seems more peaceful and less challenging. I feel so loving toward everyone. In fact, I'm open and willing to discuss topics related to our weekly spiritual development course if anyone asks me. People have started to say how much difference I make at school, but I know it's the angels working through me. I feel so connected to "all that is".

David had been working hard on his issues of abandonment and I knew this was a sign from the angels of their love and support for him. Then one week David was bursting to tell me of a very profound experience he'd had after doing the guided visualization with Archangel Chamuel and the Angels of Love.

I had begun to realize that although I can be nurturing and loving with everyone else, I haven't actually been able to love myself. There are parts of me that I actually dislike.

The meditation asks you to imagine a beautiful pink rose opening before you, and David describes how his experience affected him:

As I breathed into the music and imagined the beautiful pink colour swirling around me, as a pink rose opened in front of me, the room filled with a strong perfume of roses. My whole body experienced it; even my skin absorbed it, not just my sense of smell. I felt completely engulfed by this amazing perfume and so peaceful, calm and loved. In fact, as I went deeper into the sensation, I became aware of the absolute perfection of the rose. The perfume, the pink-coloured light surrounding me, the rose, the feeling of a "presence" about me all created a sense of love that I have never experienced before. I just knew that I was so loved, just as I am.

Many gifts are received in the form of symbols and the most common symbol of love is the rose. We can often smell roses when the angels are present and it is a spiritual gift often received during guided visualizations and meditations. When the angels give you a rose it represents a very high level of service. Each colour has a different significance: red means courage and fortitude, yellow is for wisdom and friendship, white is for purity, and pink symbolizes universal love.

Learning to love yourself

One of our greatest difficulties as humans seems to be loving ourselves as who we really are. So, learning to truly love yourself is one of the greatest gifts you can give yourself.

Here is a guided visualization you might like to do to enhance your ability to truly love yourself, as the angels do. Chamuel, the archangel who works with the powerful pink flame of love, will help you to bring more love into your life. If you would like to work with crystals for this exercise, then rose quartz is the crystal to enhance the effect of working with loving energy. Please do not make the mistake of thinking that becoming more loving will turn you into a human "doormat". Talk of love and enhancing feelings of loving energy is not a weakness. By increasing your tolerance you are not adopting a sickly sweetness. The angels are warriors of the Light; there is nothing weak about them. Real love is strong and supportive. It means loving without the need to control others, allowing them to be free. It means nurturing without smothering, and it means being true to your soul.

You can ask for Archangel Chamuel's assistance to enable you to experience self-love and dissolve the feelings of low self-esteem. He will also help you to find true love in personal relationships. True love is automatically attracted into your life once you begin to practise tolerance and gratitude in your everyday living.

Meditation for Love

It is no coincidence that pink is the colour of love and the heart chakra. All shades of pink represent love, both human and divine. The very deepest cerise is said to represent the colour of the Christ energy.

- Begin by sitting comfortably in a quiet space, where you may light a pink candle symbolizing the light of God and the angels.
- Focusing on your feet, begin slowly to scan your body so that you become aware of relaxing any tension in your muscles with every breath.
- Imagine a beautiful, pink, misty light swirling around your feet, up through your legs, abdomen and chest, rising slowly with every breath, until the pink light completely surrounds and enfolds you. The pink light leaves only love and positive energy.
- Call on Archangel Chamuel and the Angels of Love to come close to you. Let go completely of any sense of unworthiness or lack of self-love, knowing that you are totally loved and valued by God and the angels. The angels invite you to step forward into their radiant light. Feel the warmth of the rays of love from their hearts as they surround you.
- Imagine a beautiful rose bush in front of you. See the whole bush with its roots going into the ground and its bright green leaves and stems bearing perfectly formed roses.
- One of the angels reaches out and picks a rose, offering it to you. This gift represents the unity of your heart with the angel's. It is a promise of everlasting love and support. As you take the rose, thank the angels from your heart and stay for a moment in a feeling of love and total acceptance.
- Watch as the rose begins slowly to unfurl, petal by petal. Keep watching as it opens to the light, to the air. Visualize the perfection in the soft, velvety petals.

Imagine the delicate perfume. Notice the beauty and intensity of the colour.

- As the rose opens you can feel your own heart opening. Something within you begins to change, to become more receptive, more loving.
- Look into the very centre of the rose, where its life is most intense, and visualize a drop of dew forming. The light is sparkling and shining like a diamond.
- As you watch the drop of water, notice whether a message emerges for you in the form of a picture or a feeling, or perhaps hear the whisper of a word in your head. Let it emerge spontaneously without thinking. The image will represent something beautiful and meaningful that the angels want to bring into your life. Stay with that image for a while.
- Now releasing the angels with gratitude to other duties, breathe yourself slowly back into the moment and, when you are ready, open your eyes.

This light, in your heart, is with you always. Whenever your self-esteem is low, or you are tempted to be too harsh on yourself or others, reconnect to this beautiful rose light in your heart and suffuse your energy with it, calling again on the assistance of the angels of Chamuel.

You are a beautiful, unique human being, loved for yourself, created and fashioned with love by the one Creator. You are a part of the divine plan. Why would you not be loved?

"I give and receive love unconditionally."

CHAPTER 2

GIFTS OF PROTECTION

The angels have been given to us as a gift of protection. Their presence is described in many different ways, from a sensation to an actual visible appearance, often in human guise. Archangel Michael and his angels will protect your life on many levels, some of which we may not understand intellectually although we may comprehend them physically, emotionally, psychically and spiritually. Learn how to recognize these gifts of protection by sharing some of the inspiring stories of people who have experienced them for themselves.

"He has commanded His angels concerning us... to protect us in all our ways."

PSALM 91

There is no mistaking the power of angels. They appear worldwide in many religious and cultural belief systems, in one form or another. You may believe in angels as a result of your religious background; angels appear in prayers, psalms and rituals in faiths such as the Jewish, Christian and Muslim. Or your interest may have been filtered through ideas of New Age spirituality. Whatever your beliefs, there is no mistaking the power and protection available from the realms of our celestial cousins, the angels.

Once you have experienced the protection and powerful energy of the angels, especially Archangel Michael, your life will change, whether you are aware of it or not. Your personal experience leaves an indelible imprint, a realization deep within your soul. You know you have been in the presence of angels and no one has the power to be able to convince you otherwise.

Archangel Michael

In 1998, when I started to research the angels for my workshop material and my first book, *Discovering Angels*, Archangel Michael was one of the few angels to be found in any documentation. Represented throughout biblical history as the captain of the angelic hosts, and portrayed by the master craftsmen down the ages as a knight in armour, slaying a mighty dragon, everything about Michael has always contained great power and might. Michael is the all-powerful bearer of the blue flame, the sword-bearer, the protector of the meek, the champion of truth and justice. It is perhaps significant that Pope Pius XII declared St Michael the patron saint of police in 1950, protecting the "boys in blue", who in turn are protecting us.

There is so much written about Michael now. There are numerous books full of channelled messages from Michael written by authors and teachers from around the world. Many of the spiritual healers that I know now work with his healing presence during their sessions with clients, particularly in the healing that is now very popular – Reiki.

When I was first attuned to the Reiki/Seichem methods of healing over a decade ago, I was surprised when a vision of Michael appeared to me, in the form of a vivid blue light and powerful presence, accompanying Master Jesus as one my healing guides. I was teaching on a retreat in Crete, which has a strong healing energy and is believed by followers of Theosophical teachings to be the ashram, or centre of heightened spiritual activity, for the ascended master Hilarion. This is a highly evolved being working with Archangel Raphael in the heavenly realms of the green ray of healing and spiritual discovery.

There are probably as many healers who call upon the presence of Archangel Michael to assist their healing, as there are those who call upon him to give them protection. I sense that all of the archangels and angels work with us when we call, in whatever capacity they are needed. All angels can act as healers, guides, protectors and guardians. They all represent aspects of creation, the Divine, God by any name, the essence of pure Love that reaches out to us the instant our soul calls for help. This, however we understand it, is how the spirit of healing, protection and guidance actually works. It matters little which angel brings those qualities to you.

We sometimes get confused about the names we have given to angels, and whether we are calling the "right" one. The name to which we attach such importance is actually a vibration. You will attract the vibration of the quality you require at the very moment it is needed.

In an old and beautiful book called *The Beloved Archangels Speak* (channelled and written in 1953) the archangels describe how their help comes to us, and my understanding of it is this:

Angels are around us all the time. They know us well. They feel our pain, they understand our fears and our joy. Angels, as pure love and representations of the divine creative energy, are omnipresent. When something happens to make us cry out – from the soul – whether we have physically screamed or not, the angels hear us on that very out-breath. Their assistance is instantaneous; it comes back to us on the next intake of breath. Sometimes this is as a physical sensation, other times as a sense of immediately knowing what to do. Whether we act on that impulse or simply rationalize it away as a coincidence, depends on our knowledge, our own understanding of our spirituality and our belief system.

Importance of vibrations

Each of us has a unique frequency, a vibration, a spiritual essence, which I believe resonates with one or more of the angels and archangels. This is also the vibration we can feel in other human beings, too. We know instinctively whether we are comfortable in the presence of another person by their vibration and this can happen whether the vibration is higher or lower than our own. This feeling is at the root of the saying, "being on the same wavelength", or of liking someone's "energy". We feel the other person's vibration within our own aura. Sometimes we are completely happy with what we feel and at other times we are not. I am certain that we will all have had the experience of someone who makes us feel uneasy; perhaps we react by simply stepping back and creating more space between us.

It is this instinctive sensing of another's vibration or energy that initially protects us. It is part of that aspect of our self that we call discernment, our inner knowing. It is sometimes expressed as a warning, a sensing of danger about a situation, a person or someone's integrity. Some of us have excellent powers of discernment; others need extra protection from the angels while they learn.

Asking for protection

How can we protect ourselves? There are many ways, all of them simple. We can make practising protection part of a daily routine. First, you must learn to ask the angels for protection.

- As soon as you wake up, call upon Archangel Michael and the angels for protection for your home, your loved ones and yourself.
- As you get out of bed imagine you are stepping into an invisible yet impenetrable bubble of light.
- Visualize the bubble rising up around and over you, so that everywhere you go you are protected

> by an enormous and very beautiful protective layer. Arrows of harsh words and other negative psychic energies will simply slip down the surface of the bubble harmlessly.

Another effective method is to imagine you are wearing a protective cloak of blue or carrying the sword and shield of Michael's angels.

My favourite method, especially if I anticipate possible confrontation, is to imagine that I am standing under a blue spotlight. Everywhere I go the spotlight follows, just like a stage light, protecting me completely in Michael's blue flame.

Mark's story

There are so many wonderful stories about people being protected by angels and, as we know, angels can appear in many guises. Sometimes they seem to appear in human form, as in this next story, which happened some years ago to Mark, an actor friend.

It was during an exceptionally lean period of acting and I was scratching around for funds. I was so hard up at that point that I didn't have the money to pay my rent.

I lived in a three-storey Georgian house in Bristol that at the time was in need of some exterior decoration. In exchange for a month's rent I agreed to paint the outside of the house.

The weather was not good but at least it was dry, so I borrowed a ladder, bought the materials and started to paint. The lower areas were fairly straightforward and I was able to move along with the job quite quickly. I'm an actor, not a painter and decorator, and it had not occurred to me that the ladder was slightly too short for the height of the building. Being artistic rather than practical, I didn't think about the correct angle for placing the ladder safely.

I climbed to the top of the ladder. As the day progressed and I carried on with the painting I didn't really notice that the weather had turned a little too windy to be safe.

I stretched across to paint a section of the wall at arm's length and just as I did that the wind caught my ladder so that it started to swing backward, away from the wall. Time went into slow motion, as I felt the ladder sway and dropped the paintbrush and paint. I literally saw my life "pass before my very eyes" and felt certain that this was the end for me (or at the very least I would be badly injured). I closed my eyes and held on for dear life, saying under my breath, "Oh God, help." Suddenly I felt that the ladder had stopped moving.

When I dared to open my eyes and look down, a very tall man was holding the lower end of ladder and pushing it back toward the wall of the house. He was a well-dressed bearded Indian man wearing a turban.

As I stumbled down the ladder I literally felt sick at the thought of what might have happened had this stranger not stepped in and held it for me; I couldn't believe my luck! I hurried down the ladder as the man held it safely. Once on the ground I thanked the stranger profusely and was told firmly that I should take more care of myself.

Taking the ladder from the stranger, I moved it away from the base of the wall to a safer angle. Then I turned to speak to him, but he had already disappeared without another word. I looked up and down in both directions, but the gentleman was nowhere to be seen. I now tell this story of how I nearly died with the conviction that this was definitely an angel who had appeared at that moment to save my life.

Caroline's story

Caroline is one of my students who wrote and told me this story about how Michael's angels protected her in a troubled area of Belfast, Northern Ireland.

My friends and I have twice-weekly angel meetings when we read about angels, ground ourselves, listen to guided meditations, read angel cards, study archangels and ascended masters and generally have a calm and peaceful time. However, the place where we hold our meetings is in one of Belfast's interface areas (which separate the two religious communities). We are a cross-community group and enjoy nights out together and I know it sounds silly, given the nature of what we do, to say religion doesn't come into the equation, but we don't get into the debate of personal religion.

One night last year only Theresa and I made it to the meeting as there had been rioting in the area and most people were nervous of venturing out in the evening. We went ahead anyway and naturally invoked the protection of the Archangel Michael. We had a lovely night. When we left we noticed the road was eerily quiet, although there were a few small groups of youths who seemed to be roaming about looking for "fun".

Now we live on either side of the divide here (between Protestant and Catholic areas) and the place where we had to part to go home was a well-known trouble spot.

But as we got to the crossroads to go our separate ways we noticed three men standing at corners of the crossroads. For some reason we both assumed they were policemen as they appeared to be wearing some kind of uniform. As we got up to them they nodded and smiled.

We parted company and hurried home. As soon as I arrived I rang Theresa as I realized something strange had happened. We both agreed that the three "police" were not wearing the modern uniform, but a very old-fashioned style, now completely out of date. There were no police vehicles in sight and foot police were almost unheard of in that area.

We gratefully concluded that not only had we made it home safely but we'd had the total protection of Archangel Michael's angels. We decided that this was definitely an angelic intervention, whoever the three strange uniformed men had been. How grateful we were, and I can honestly say we always ask Him to look after us, and He always does.

Keith's story

It is not always a passing stranger who saves the day. Angelic protection can come in many forms.

A couple of years ago I was a passenger in a car and we were travelling along a fairly quiet road, at some speed. I suddenly gasped at the appearance of what seemed to me to look like the "grim reaper" before me. He appeared to be coming from my side and I could see him in great detail. I could see his black cape, black wings dark burning eyes and I could even make out strange patterns all over his face. I was so alarmed and shocked that my gasp unnerved the driver, who automatically slowed down. Within a few seconds of witnessing the apparition, a car suddenly sped toward us, from nowhere, coming out of a turning at great speed. But because we were able to swerve, the driver missed us by a hair's breadth. We most certainly would have been killed if we had been going any faster.

I'm not sure what kind of angel it was. Or even, perhaps, if it was the Angel of Death, although it saved our lives, rather than took them. Wherever it came from I know it was spiritual in some way and I took it as a warning. I have really tried hard since to make sure I live my life to the best of my ability. I certainly believe in the protection of angels. I suppose they have to appear in a way that is powerful enough to make you aware of their presence.

Denise's story

Prevention of car accidents has often been attributed to guardian angels. The majority of stories I receive are from grateful believers who have narrowly avoided a terrible car accident.

A few years ago I was in quite a severe car accident. It was terrible weather. I had pulled out of a junction, but the wheels of the car got stuck in the mud. I saw another car coming fast toward me, so I put my foot full on the accelerator and began to move, though nowhere near fast enough. I knew that the other car was going too fast to stop. I urgently prayed for help and as I watched I saw a wondrous sight.

Everything appeared to me in slow motion and I could see forms of light moving like a tug-of-war team. There was a stream of light holding on to the other car, slowing it down. I could feel the other car as it struck mine. Then I could feel the sides of my car being pushed in, but somehow I was not afraid. I was rescued by the fire brigade and taken to hospital.

Although in shock and sporting a cracked collar bone, I was absolutely fine. A few days later I saw my car. I stared in absolute disbelief at my driver's seat, which had been pushed over to the passenger side of the car. I was told that the car was thrown over 100ft, yet I had not felt the impact. I know I am so lucky to be alive and I thank my angels all the time for this. I know without a shadow of doubt that they saved my life.

Near-death experiences

Near-death has an enormous effect on one's psyche and, not surprisingly, scientists like to try to prove that our "spiritual" experience is merely a chemical imbalance within the brain caused by the impact of high levels of adrenalin, due to fear. Even if they are right, or if this is partly true, these "angelic" life-saving moments still have a profound effect on our remaining journey through life.

I am greatly privileged that so many people have shared their feelings with me about those times when, if it had not been for the intervention of angels, and in particular Michael, they would not be alive now to tell the tale. Some of these people went on to do great things with their lives.

One such person who had a life-saving experience, a friend and co-angel worker, has since helped many others find their spiritual purpose.

Darren's story

Darren Linton, a fellow angel facilitator and author, believes that he wouldn't be alive today were it not for the angels – they saved him from a terrible car crash.

Over the last decade, the angels have worked through Darren and other light workers, who have, through a divine connection to the angels, been able to touch and help thousands of people all over the world. By tuning in to the angelic messages and offering to be of a high level of service to God and humanity as angelic ambassadors on earth, people have received healing, guidance, love, inspiration and a multitude of blessings from the angels, which have enriched and in many cases, transformed their lives.

Darren has been working with the angels for over ten years now. He believes that the angels selected him to be one of their ambassadors on earth, to help spread their light and to assist people everywhere in connecting with their angels.

I used to commute to work on the M25, a busy motorway. I would get into the fast lane and stay there until I reached my turn-off. One day, I was driving fast and I noticed a truck matching my speed in the lane next to me. I didn't think anything of this. Then a voice in my head said, "Overtake this truck and change lanes. Do this NOW." Without thinking, I felt a force press down on my accelerator foot and the car shot forward. I checked I had passed the truck and changed lanes. Just then, something flashed by me, apparently going in the wrong direction in the lane I had just been in. I looked round to discover that a large truck had broken down in that lane.

I had been hurtling toward a stationary truck at high speed, with another truck next to me, so that I couldn't swerve. Had it not been for the intervention, I would be dead. At the time, I thought "Phew! That was lucky!" I was somewhat shaken, but shrugged it off as one of those near misses, and thought, "Someone up there is looking after me". We often have experiences like that – near misses, lucky escapes. It wasn't until years later, when I was talking with angels, that I realized that it was my guardian angel who had been protecting me and who had saved me.

I asked my angels "Was it you who saved me from that accident?" They said, "Of course, Loved One" (that's what they call me). "It was not your time to die. You have much work yet to do on earth." So if it wasn't for the angels, I wouldn't be here. As I was to discover later, they had big plans for my life. I feel they had selected me to help them to spread their work."

Amanda's story

Amanda, one of my recent workshop participants, tells a story of her near-death experience in water.

I must have been three at the time, as my dad was still alive but very ill (he left us shortly after my fourth birthday). We had all gone away on a summer holiday, to a holiday camp. I suppose it was a last holiday together. My mum had taken me out and I can remember that I was wearing a homemade jumper, which I loved. We came to a swimming pool, where a boy who had lost half his arm was playing in the water. My mum told me later that I had said, "Oh, Mummy, he has lost his arm!" and

I immediately jumped in to see if I could find it. It's so funny how small children think; I thought he had dropped it and it was somewhere under the water.

Anyway, down I went and I can clearly remember going right down, deep under the water. My mum said she couldn't see me and as she cannot swim she was helpless. She became hysterical, but up I came. When I got down to the bottom of the pool a man was there and he pushed me with great force up to the surface. My mum pulled me out by my jumper, which grew longer and longer on the walk back to the chalet. My mum was so upset, but all I kept saying was, "The man pushed me up".

I know now, as an adult, that she must have thought I was mad, or at least making it up. The funny thing is that when I was a little older I saw who I thought was the same man on the television. I was watching an old programme of a comedian called Charlie Drake. I said, "That's him! That looks like the man who pushed me up out of the water." I hadn't even heard of him as a child, and I don't understand why a guardian angel would materialize as a TV comedian, but maybe a friendly little man with a round face was a little less frightening to a child. I'll never know! I only know that my reaction and such a close resemblance to someone I recognized later made the whole experience a little more believable for my mum.

Chris's story

Another water story comes from Chris, who was one of the friends I made around ten years ago when I was filming a special feature called *I Believe in Angels* for *Kilroy*, a daily morning television show. Chris shares her near-death experience willingly, knowing that it is difficult for some people to take in.

I was out on a date with a young man who lived on a houseboat, moored by a jetty. It was a cold evening in February and having been out to a concert I decided to go back to his boat, which was cosy and warm, although I actually have a morbid fear of the water.

As we walked along the wooden walkway I tripped over a rope, slipped and fell into the water. I was terrified and completely panicked as I fell, sinking straight beneath the surface. I held my breath, but being unable to swim I couldn't seem to lift myself up in the water at all. It didn't help that I was wearing a winter coat and boots. It was freezing cold. I was helpless and I felt I was going to drown. Then I heard a voice say to me, "Breathe, you will be fine". Of course I could not breathe – I was under water – but the voice kept on urging me to breathe. It was a calm male voice and I realized I had heard it before many times in my meditations. It was the voice of my guardian angel, whom I called John.

In the meantime my friend was running about trying to find me and throwing ropes and lifebelts into the water. There were no mobile phones in those days and he had to resort to running to get help. He thought I had surely drowned as there was no sign of me and I had been under water for about ten minutes.

The voice of my guardian angel John continued to speak to me reassuringly and very slowly I felt myself floating upward to the surface. I was pulled out, an ambulance arrived and I was rushed to the nearest hospital and treated for shock. People often dispute that I was under the water for so long, or that I could have been "breathing". Nevertheless I am here now to tell the tale and if I hadn't been protected by my guardian angel I don't believe I would be.

Chris, a registered nurse and counsellor for many years, carried on to work with groups and individuals, encouraging and facilitating their connection with their own guardian angels.

Angel sentries

Because we can also ask the angels to protect our property, it is quite usual for "angel lovers" to place a blue light of protection around their home or car, when they leave it unattended. I have made this a practice whenever I am away.

At one stage I had a fifth-floor apartment in east London. I loved living there. I enjoyed the brightness and light of the place: its high ceiling, beautiful calm energy and the amazing views over the city. My large balcony was always suffused with colour from my favourite bright-red geraniums, which seemed to grow all year round. When I left one April to go to New Zealand for three weeks, I asked a friend to water my houseplants for me and collect any mail. As I left and stood by the door of my flat to lock it, I called upon Michael to place sentries outside, and off I went.

In dependable style, my friend, Iren, arrived at my apartment about a week after my departure, as promised. She stopped at my door and, as she lifted her key to the lock, she felt frozen to the spot by a sudden strange and powerful presence by her side. As she turned, in a flash she saw an enormous column of light to the left of my door. She stood, alarmed, for a couple of seconds, and then intuitively understood what she had witnessed. "It's absolutely fine," she said to the invisible guardian at my door, "I'm only here to water the plants; I won't disturb the energy." She felt comfortable to enter, but later told me that she was certain no intruder would have been able to pass the angel-protector of my door.

Claire's story

I had experienced the invisible supernatural protective force of something greater than me many times in my life, so was not surprised when my daughter started telling me about her "visitor".

When she was young, Claire slept in a bunkbed above a cupboard in her tiny room. Sometimes, when I went in to say goodnight, she would tell me, from under her bed covers, "The Indian lady is here again!" Claire could see a small sari-clad woman standing in the corner of her room. Often the woman would be on the upstairs landing and Claire became very nervous, refusing to go to her bedroom on her own.

By her pillow she had a picture of her own guardian angel pinned to the wall, drawn by her grandma (my mother), and, just like me as a child, she had a strong belief that Jesus was her friend. I reassured her that the lady meant her no harm, but at that time had very little knowledge of how to deal with unwelcome visitors of the spiritual variety. I told her to try to ask the lady what she wanted, but Claire was too scared. I told her to ask the lady to go away because she was frightening, and to ask Jesus and her angels to keep her safe. Claire's daddy didn't believe in "all that nonsense" and told her very reassuringly that it was all in her imagination, probably because she read too many horror stories with her friends. Claire's visitor went away.

Some time later a psychic intuitive friend of my mother's came to London from the USA and I knew she would be able to help. I asked her to go through the house and tell me whether she could see or feel any spiritual presence (I had not discussed Claire's experiences beforehand). "Yes," she said in a very matter-of-fact manner, after spending a while moving around the bedrooms and hallway, "there is a small Indian woman, in spirit, standing outside the bathroom, wearing a yellow sari. She has been sent as a guardian to watch over Claire. It seems she may need some help at some stage soon."

A soothing presence

What a pity that "We don't know what it is we don't know, until we realize we didn't know it"! There is never a good time for a family to fall apart. In Claire's case her father had agreed to move out, but at the last moment refused, thus forcing me to be the one to go. There was no chance of reconciliation and Claire didn't want to leave her home and friends, so even though she felt anxious she stayed behind with her brother and father. She was fifteen.

One night, feeling very depressed, she woke from a fretful sleep to sense a heavy darkness approaching her; a suffocating, dense, negative presence, which spread closer and closer, until she could feel it pressing down on her chest. Instantly and instinctively she prayed for help and a bright white light appeared in her room, easing the pressure of the darkness on her chest. "Are you sure this is what you want, Claire?" said a gentle, soothing female voice. "Let me show you something." Claire saw a vision of her father sitting in his office, leaning on his desk with his head in his hands, weeping. Then she saw her mum sitting on her bed in her new flat. She had spread old photographs of her children, whom she so loved, over the bed and was looking through them. Claire saw that her mum was silently sobbing.

Next she saw a vision of her older brother, Daniel, in his room, also looking through old photos and this time she could see over his shoulder that they were pictures of them both having fun as children. She realized, with a pang of horror, that they were all grieving her own death. Tears poured down her cheeks as she felt their pain. "Oh no. Please help me," she whispered, "I don't want this to happen." "Then I'll protect you," said the voice.

With that, Claire saw the light immediately expand throughout her room and the darkness pull away like a moving shadow. At the foot and sides of her bed she saw the shape of three tall men, with what she described as golden light around them, stretching between them. She knew that they were angels. Although she didn't dare to turn around in case he was looking at her, she knew there was a fourth angel right behind her head.

Claire rang me and we met the very next day so that she could tell me about it in detail. She had been very depressed and unhappy, but had met a lovely boyfriend, who was helping her through her upheaval. I couldn't explain it at the time, other than to reassure her that she could now believe without any doubt that she was being looked after by angels. She certainly need never be afraid of the dark again.

Since then Claire's life has brought many dark and painful challenges, some of which have been dangerous, including a battle with diabetes that almost took her life. Perhaps in some way the visits of her silent Indian guardian and the vision of that night, twelve years ago, were to prepare her and show how, even in the depths of despair, her celestial guardians are with her, always. She has become highly intuitive and accepts quite pragmatically that everything is "always as it is meant to be".

As with Claire's story, time after time we are shown that the light is angelic divine power and will protect and guide us, regardless of whether the outcome matches our human expectations. It doesn't really matter whether we understand this or not. In fact, I often think that the mystery of not knowing has more impact.

Jackie and Brian's story

Over two thousand years ago there was a very important sect within the Jewish community called the Essenes (see page 15), who believed in and communed with, two distinct orders of angels: the Angels of the Heavenly Father and the Angels of the Earthly Mother. Today, the groups of people who follow these regular communions are called the Essene Network. Without angels watching over Jackie and Brian Stevenson, there might not have been an Essene Network for us to belong to.

Years ago, before Jackie and Brian were married, there were fewer private phones and no mobiles, so people often had to go out to a public phone box to call their friends. One evening Jackie had returned home after chatting on the phone to her boyfriend Brian, then a student. Suddenly she felt the need to go back and call him again, even though she did not have anything urgent to say to him. Jackie just felt that she *really* needed to speak to him. She told me she had the sensation of eyes boring into her spine and it gave her such a sense of urgency she rushed out of the house to the phone box to call her boyfriend again.

When the phone rang Brian's father answered and explained that Brian had gone back outside to fix his car. On Jackie's insistence his father went out to bring Brian to the phone and Jackie had to admit that she didn't really have anything specific to tell him, just that she wanted him to talk to her again. After a few moments they said their fond farewells and she replaced the receiver to return home.

The next morning, she received a call from Brian. "Thank God you rang me again last night," he told her in a near whisper. "While I was speaking to you, the car fell to the ground without its wheel. The jack collapsed under it. My legs had been under the car… Jackie I would have been underneath the car. Your call saved my legs and possibly my life!"

The Essene Network begins

Much later, Jackie and Brian, having married and raised their children, met a couple of remarkable people. One was a man now known to many as the Grandfather of the New Age, Sir George Trevelyan, and the other was Anne MacEwen, both of whom shared, with Jackie and Brian, an avid interest in the Essene teachings and way of life. Many people were becoming interested in the Essene way and they decided to form a society or network to bring the teachings of communion with angels and the hidden words of Jesus into the open, as a way of life, for others. At the time, twelve people were interested in forming a society and it was decided to meet at Anne's flat in Bath.

It was a small room, and the group members would have much to say. Brian, Jackie and Anne were worried about how long this first meeting would take, and even wondered about the wisdom of forming such a large group to decide anything. They prayed for help and asked the angels to guide those who needed to be there to come along. Gradually, for one reason or another, every member of the group rang with their excuses. Even Sir George was involved in such heavy traffic that it wasn't worth his while coming.

The angels saved the day! The three of them held their first meeting, decided on a name and formed the Essene Network International (ENI). Without laborious discussion or conflicting ideas they harmoniously created the network, which has now been growing steadily for over twenty years.

Suzanna's story

Suzanna is a member of the Essene group and an avid believer in angels. She is a warm and glamorous lady, whose long career in the fashion business has included modelling in the studio and on the catwalk. Her working life has given her many years on and off film sets and she has developed a great sense of fun as well as a love of the sacred. Her belief in angels has helped her through many sticky situations and here she tells of an accident in which she believes she could have been seriously injured if not for the intervention of angelic guardians.

It was early morning and I was hurrying across London to a film set to work as an extra. There were problems on the London Underground and I had to change lines several times. I was carrying a rather bulky rucksack and two holdalls and as I hurried through one of the stations I became anxious at the prospect of being late. I didn't want to lose my job on set. I reached the top of the escalator and because I was in such a rush I literally leapt on, stepping awkwardly and misjudging the weight and size of my rucksack. Looking down from the top of a high escalator, I felt myself falling. I screamed. Instantly and incredibly an almighty force stopped me. It was like a huge hand pushing me sideways and making me sit down abruptly on the escalator steps.

Bruised and shaken, but feeling very grateful, Suzanna continued her journey and enjoyed the day's work, happily telling everyone of her miraculous "fall". When she arrived home that night she laughed as she emptied her bags. To her great surprise, there in the bottom of her shoulder bag had mysteriously appeared a large fluffy white feather, a keepsake reminder of her angelic protector.

The angels may save our physical bodies in times of danger, but they can also protect us spiritually and on a psychic level, too. There is a fine line between psychic paranormal events and the spiritual, and sometimes it is difficult to differentiate between the two. Have a look at these next two stories.

Denise's story

Denise, a gifted healer, wrote to say:

One night I received a phone call from a woman I had helped once before; she asked if I could help a child who was "seeing" spirits and was terrified as the spirits seemed angry and violent toward her. The child's mother had already been in contact with a professional medium, but she was so busy that she could not see her for a fortnight. Gratefully the mother booked her. In the meantime and in despair, I was contacted. I told the worried mother that I would not interfere in the medium's work as it would be different to mine, but that I would pray and ask for protection from Archangel Michael for the child. I explained that I would also ask for the child's guardian angel to assist, for the child's greater good.

I received another phone call from the woman a few weeks later to tell me that since speaking to me the child had suffered no more disturbances. Furthermore, when the professional medium walked into the child's bedroom, she said it was filled with angels and asked who had been praying in that room. There was nothing for her to do as someone else had done the work. I had not left my living room. I simply asked and I received – I have never been let down. This works in all my healings and I am respectfully proud to be one of the many who have been chosen to assist in any way I can.

Louise's story

This next story is about the plight of my neighbour, Louise. It offers a clear demonstration of the mysterious paranormal intervention that we attribute to the angels. Louise is a firm believer in angels and, as is often the case between friends, we formed a strong bond even though she is much younger than me. With powerful psychic gifts of her own, she and a friend had been running a psychic development circle, which is where she met her partner. When she moved in next door and we met, we were both delighted to have a common interest in angels and the spiritual life and had great conversations about the old house she now lived in, her children's psychic awareness and her interest in my books.

It happened just after midnight, when my present husband Brian and I were watching television, catching up on a recorded series we had missed. With curtains drawn, we were sitting curled up by the log fire, cosily engrossed in the latest episode, when the dog sprang to her feet. We both looked at one another and said we thought we'd heard the doorbell ring. It was quite a shock to hear the bell ring at such a late hour, especially in our quiet lane.

Brian jumped up saying, "Who on earth would ring the door at this time of night? It must be urgent!" He approached the door and peered through the glass, but there was no one there. He opened the door. No one was there, and there was no one in the lane. Then he came back to the lounge and, with a shrug, sat down to continue watching our programme.

Just as we settled the doorbell rang again. Brian went again to the door, looked out into the lane and still there was no one there. We had recently bought a wireless doorbell, which had proved rather a nuisance. Sometimes it would pick up the ring of one of the neighbouring cottages and often it would ring someone else's choice of tune, too, which could be both amusing and irritating. He looked toward the other cottage whose doorbell we sometimes heard. There was no sign of anyone. Then, just as he sat down again, mystified, it rang for the third time. This time he leapt to the door, as if to catch the culprit red-handed.

Yet again there was no one at the door. Brian came back, annoyed by now in case it was mischievous teenagers playing games. He slipped on his shoes and, leaving the door wide open, he went outside and looked up and down the lane. There was no one around. Who could have rung the bell?

Then he heard muffled voices to the left of our house, at the entrance to the fields, where people occasionally park. Curiosity got the better of him. He went over to take a closer look and immediately came back to fetch me. It was our neighbour, Louise, with her two children wrapped in duvets, with tear-stained faces and teddies in their arms. After a huge argument, her partner, in a fit of temper, had told her to leave. So, fearfully, with her two children, no money, no petrol in her car and no credit on her phone, she was about to spend the cold night, distraught, sleeping in her car, with nowhere to go.

Brian helped Louise with her bags and I brought the children in, ushered them into a spare room and tucked them up in bed. Then I went back down to put the kettle on while Brian sat Louise down by the fire to listen to her story.

A little later he walked into the kitchen, closed the door gently then turned to me, ashen-faced. "Louise didn't ring the doorbell," he whispered. "No one came near the door… neither she nor the children rang it at all… this is unbelievable. I don't understand it." He added, "Do you realize that somehow, Louise – or someone else on her behalf – made that doorbell ring…?"

Louise feels she has a psychic link to her grandmother, whom she believes is now one of her guardian angels or guides. Somehow, in some way or other, the doorbell rang. And not just once, but three times. How do we understand this phenomenon? Could it be that Louise's distress heightened her psychic energy, which called in her angels, or even her grandmother, to help her from beyond the veil? And that by means we cannot fully understand, the doorbell was rung, perhaps through electronic waves or some high-frequency vibrational energy? Or that, drawing on her own emotional charge as she walked past, Louise connected with the strong bond she and I had formed, which psychically created an electric charge between us that caused the electronic bell to ring?

I do not pretend to know the answer. Perhaps Louise somehow rang the door herself, telepathically, in her anguish and cry for help. However we try to work out an explanation, I don't doubt that it was an angelic force protecting Louise and her children by calling Brian and myself to the rescue. It was a mysterious occurrence with a satisfactory outcome, but one that has played on in Brian's mind for a very long time.

Diane's story

Angels don't only protect human beings, as Diane from Ireland tells us in this story of her dog and the angels.

The family dog is called Sid. He is a red and white Boxer and his sole purpose is to protect his family, which are myself and my children – so much so that one day he bounded over a 6ft fence to protect my youngest daughter, who was being cornered by a stray dog. Sid is big and fearless, or so I thought.

We had recently moved house and everything and everyone was upside down. I was busy attending to things and I took it for granted that Sid was fine. Never again will I think this after what I witnessed. Sid was left in the kitchen all alone in a strange house, his family too busy to look after him.

Late at night I went to make a cup of tea and as I opened the kitchen door I saw Sid sitting, looking up. All around him, in a protective embrace, was a form of cascading light against the darkness of the kitchen. An angel was giving Sid a hug. Both Sid and the angel looked at me; it seemed as if both of them smiled. I knew that I had to leave them alone. I closed the door and went to bed. Now, every so often, Sid looks up and I know that his angels are there for him.

Grandma Elsie's story

Many strange things happened to my grandmother Elsie during her life and she often related exciting tales to me as a child. I particularly liked hearing about her being saved by her rubber boots when her umbrella was struck by lightning, when my mother was only a few months old. She obviously had a reason for living on, as did my mother. My grandma often told me one of her many stories of how her life was saved and this one, about the hands in the smog, was also one of my favourites.

The North of England was always susceptible to winter smog, also known as "pea soup" fog, which was so thick it could be impossible to see any distance at all. I can remember how frightening it was to be caught outdoors as a young child in fogs like this. They would arrive with scant warning: a few misty wisps, a weird smoky smell and then suddenly everything became scarily invisible. Once a fog had fallen everyone was stuck where they were, for the duration.

My grandma Elsie was returning home after a day's work with her mother in a grocery shop in Bradford, Yorkshire. Although my mother, Sylvia, was only a few weeks old, my grandma was helping out in the build-up to Christmas. Carrying my mother wrapped in a shawl, she hurried in the late afternoon to reach home before dark. She decided to walk across country. This was her regular route, a walk of about 2 miles, which she preferred to crossing the busy city, waiting in endless bus queues.

No sooner had she started across the fields than she noticed the first wisps of fog swirling around her. Having begun the journey, she felt she had no alternative but to keep going. She could smell the coal-filled air, polluted with factory smoke, as it drifted heavily toward her. But Elsie felt safe; she knew the area of Chellor Dene well, having played in the open fields, Victorian reservoirs and the deep, wooded valley all her childhood years. A very determined and feisty lady, she had no fear. She tightened her shawl around her baby and quickened her step. Within minutes, Elsie could no longer see her foot in front of her, but confident of her footing, she kept on going.

Helping hands

Suddenly, to her great surprise, a heavy masculine hand clamped on her shoulder and forced her to the ground. In amazement she tried to get up, but again the hand forced her down and she heard a voice say, "Stay there". Unused to obeying anyone, she tried again to stand up and continue her journey, but she was unable to shake off the steady, strong hands, which she could now feel on each shoulder. Giving in to what was clearly stronger than her, she remained seated.

Disturbed by her mother's sudden movements, the baby woke up and so Elsie started singing to her. She hummed little tunes at first and then found herself singing the words from church hymns, until finally she was blasting out rousing choruses of praise and thanksgiving, as if straight from the pages of her Methodist hymn book, at the top of her voice. The fog lifted as suddenly as it had fallen, and laughing in amusement at the sound of her own muffled voice echoing around the valley, she stood up and straightened her clothes to continue home.

Then, as she bent to pick up her bag, to her absolute horror she discovered that she was less than 1ft away from the deep ravine that runs through the area. Another bold step forward and she would have almost certainly fallen over the edge, with my mother in her arms. Something, or someone, had saved their lives.

Decades later, whenever she told me the story (even though I had heard it dozens of times, to my quivering delight, as a child) she always puzzled whether it had been the spirit of her grandfather, or a guardian angel, who had saved her. Either way, she certainly lived to tell the tale, and with gratitude in my heart I say, "thank goodness for that!"

Positive thoughts

The stories of protection are endless. We human beings are strong, courageous, intelligent and proud. Yet we do need to be protected, often from our own destructive behaviour. The most effective method of protection is unbelievably simple and yet elusive: think positive, loving thoughts. The Law of the Universe demands that "like attracts like", so loving and positive thoughts attract positivity. Fed by the emotion of love and gratitude they grow, until everything becomes positive and loving. It is all down to personal choice and attitude. Only you can control your thoughts. Thinking positive, loving thoughts creates a wide and beautiful protective aura around you. It also follows that if your world is harmonious, you attract harmonious and loving people, including the angels, into your life.

Meditation for Grounding and Protection

- Just for a moment close your eyes and breathe deeply into your abdomen. Imagine a beautiful, bright, almost fluorescent blue light surrounding you.

- Call upon Archangel Michael to send his Angels of Protection to be by your side. Imagine the blue light permeating you in a swirling motion that soothes and empowers you. Feel yourself becoming taller, your spine and neck straightening, your crown opening.
- As you breathe the blue light down through your crown, imagine it slowly filling your body and working its way down through your feet into the ground below you.
- Visualize the light forming a beautiful protective bubble around you and allow yourself to trust in the powerful protective force of the angelic light.
- Thank the angels and, breathing down into your lower abdomen, grounding the energy, bring yourself back into the moment, knowing that you are fully protected, psychically, physically and spiritually.

"I am protected by a shield of angelic power,
and nothing can harm me."

CHAPTER 3

GIFTS OF HEALING

We tend to think that "healing" is all about broken bodies and diseases, yet Archangel Raphael's angelic healing shows that it can take the form of healing rifts between family members or friends, or conflict in projects, memories, places, financial predicaments and a great many other circumstances. Our thoughts are so powerful that they can create negative energy that causes our emotional and physical illness. How wonderful that by strengthening our connection to the energies of the angels we may heal our bodies, our relationships and, most importantly, transform and heal our thoughts.

"The angels can heal the moment, the day and sometimes your entire life."

Contrary to popular belief, it is not essential to call upon a specific angel to bring about healing. Many of us have healing guides and angels for healing, and others work directly with God, or Spirit, who channels universal healing energy through them. However, the different angels and their identities may be confusing. What is important is that we focus attention and intention on the highest possible outcome for every situation, calling upon the angels of the healing project or issue at hand, regardless of whether we know their names or not. I personally felt drawn to seven named archangels, who seem to be appropriate for my own teaching and healing methods.

Working with Raphael

One of the seven archangels I often call upon to be with me and bless each interaction throughout my day is Raphael, whose name means "God heals". Along with the Archangel Gabriel, Raphael works closely with anyone who has chosen to serve in caring and healing professions. Not surprisingly he is also the guardian of travel, particularly exploration. As a guide in self-discovery, Raphael can be called to help us to uncover truths about ourselves along our spiritual journey.

From many different perspectives we can view healing as a divine gift of grace. When we are sick, out of sorts and "dis-eased", there is always an emotional imbalance or mental issue related to the pain and discomfort. When we are faced with something uncomfortable in our lives, we may well avoid the issue causing the discomfort. It may often be suppressed, or suppressed *and* ignored, for a very long time. Awareness of the underlying reasons for the discomfort gives us a chance to change, and if we choose to change we then accept the "gift" within the illness. The silver lining to the cloud of discomfort or pain (whether emotional or physical) is that, with guidance, we *can* heal.

Sometimes we can do it on our own, by a process of elimination and determination. More usually we need to ask for help and healing. The help can come to us directly from God as a message of wisdom and enlightenment, to which, when we search deep within our soul, we can find the clues that enable us to release the negative thought patterns that are at the root of the problem.

During my shifts at the nursing home and hospice, I would ask Raphael to use me in any appropriate way to bring healing, whether through a smile, gentle touch or by simply using the right words to bring comfort. In an environment of palliative care, working with the elderly and dying, the angels' gift of bringing comfort on physical, emotional and spiritual levels to others became an essential part of my day.

Raphael has certainly been a great influence on my life in past years. He is not only the great healing archangel but is also said to work with the ascended masters of scientific discovery. In this role he enables humanity by revealing and uncovering universal truths about the workings of the cosmos and our beautiful planet earth. Raphael continually shares gifts with us on many levels of understanding, particularly in discovering – and rediscovering – new and ancient medicinal cures. It is said that it was Raphael who gave Noah a huge volume of knowledge, called the Book of Raziel, containing all the cures he would need for himself, his family and all the animals on the Ark.

The role of coincidence

Help might come to us by means of a change in direction such as a letting go of a toxic relationship or our immediate environment, which may literally be making us sick. And, very often, the healing might come to us via a friend or guide, who just turns up at the right moment "out of the blue"; someone who has been sent to us by the angelic realms in synchronistic circumstances that we like to call "just a coincidence".

Coincidences like this certainly occurred in my life during a long period of chronic back pain, ongoing gynaecological problems and spiralling depression, which I did not understand (at the time) were related to emotional insecurity and unhappiness. Trying to run a business and cope with my difficult personal life, I felt a total wreck. One day, someone I was talking to gave me a copy of a book by Shakti Gawain called *Living in the Light*. This inspired me deeply and, with the realization that I would have to take full responsibility for my life, I began to search even more frantically for a way out of my emotional fog.

My way out materialized through the receptionist at my osteopath's practice, who shared my interest in angels and the supernatural. She suggested I visited a spiritual healer and then told me about a psychic fair that was being held that very afternoon. I was very reluctant, but she was unperturbed and because she felt psychically guided to encourage and help me, she insisted on taking me there herself.

A chance encounter

I wandered slowly past each of the exhibitors, wondering which one I should go to. I had only limited money and, being conscious of my husband's disapproval, I wanted to be careful how I used my cash. Because I was already familiar with numerology (my mother had been using Pythagorean numerology for years) I was drawn to a kindly looking man offering numerology and tarot readings. The accuracy of his words shocked me. He told me many things relating to my personality and life: the date I had married, how many children I had and their gender, and that I was a nurse but not using my healing skills. He told me that I was deeply spiritual and would, indeed, write books eventually, and then he stopped and looked concerned. After a few moments of silence he explained that there are universal laws attached to his "gift", to which a good psychic must adhere. He told me that he had a dilemma because he had seen something that he knew he should tell me about, but that it would be painful for me to hear. He had stopped for a few minutes, he said, so that he could go "within" to ask for spiritual guidance and make a decision about what to do next.

A catalyst

What he then told me was a monumental catalyst in changing my life. He explained that the numbers showed him that my work life and home life were too convoluted. The cards and numbers, which he was interpreting clairvoyantly, revealed that there was something very unhealthy in my relationship at work, which was dramatically affecting my family (my husband and I were running a business together, causing stress and arguments) and that I was allowing myself to be bullied. His considered advice was that I should change the situation and find another occupation to suit my nature. Troubled by what he saw, he warned that if I did not do something immediately it would be extremely detrimental to my health. He also warned me that it was affecting my children. Something had to change, straightaway. And indeed it did all change.

What if?

But, what if I had not had an emergency appointment that morning with my osteopath and what if that particularly friendly receptionist had not been on duty? What if the psychic fair had been somewhere else? What if I had not been drawn to visit that particular numerologist? I wonder how much longer I would have procrastinated. Is there such a thing as divine timing? Gifts from the angels? I know so!

By the time I came to be working at the nursing home and the hospice I had already done a short course in healing with the angels, and this complemented my nursing skills very well. However, there was always an awareness of unwritten universal laws that guided me away from "imposing" healing energy on anyone who had not asked for it. My role was just to be available as a conduit, or vessel, and allow the healing energy to flow through me, should the need arise. Time after time

I became aware of opportunities to serve in this way, sharing the divine gift of angelic healing with others.

Skip's story

One day a friend in Guernsey fell and badly broke his elbow. He was already in his sixties. The doctor told him that the healing process would be lengthy and that his plaster would be removed in six weeks to check progress, but that it would probably take a further six weeks to heal after that. Skip had grown up in the Welsh valleys and was familiar with charismatic Christianity and the concept of "healing hands". I asked him if he would like to experiment with me in some daily angel healing and he readily agreed.

I concentrated on my friend and his fracture during my meditation and asked Archangel Raphael to help us to mend his arm. My angelic healing teacher offered to help, too, and the three of us agreed that we would all work at midday, every day. As we two called the angels closer and connected in mind (wherever we were at midday), we concentrated our thoughts and attention on sending loving healing to my friend's arm, while he, at the same time, stopped and concentrated his thoughts on the loving healing light being sent to him. I asked him to visualize the energy as a bright light surrounding and healing the broken bone and tissue of his damaged arm.

An amazing result

Six weeks later the plaster came off for a progress check. The consultant was more than surprised that for "a man of his age" his arm had healed so quickly. X-rays showed that the bone had completely knitted and, instead of having the plaster on for a further six weeks, all he needed was some physiotherapy to strengthen the muscles around the fracture. Of course, Skip was over the moon. "I can't believe it," he told me. "This is amazing! The plaster is off, the consultant was intrigued – especially when I told him I was receiving distant healing. Your angels certainly have done the trick!" And I had my confirmation that focused distant healing, especially magnified by the mystical power of three, really does work.

In all the excitement and enthusiasm of my new spiritual discoveries, coincidences and synchronistic meetings at that time, I was keen to prove the angelic healing techniques to myself (and everybody else) whenever possible. My experience was fairly new and I needed to establish that this healing gift was not actually "of" me but "through" me, in close connection to the healing angels. Those who have trained in spiritual healing, in whatever form, will understand my lack of confidence and the need to test myself continually, and the energy flowing through me, until I gained total trust. I was given countless opportunities at that time.

Vera's story

As any nurse working with the elderly and dying will tell you, it is impossible not to develop a fondness for some of the long-term patients, regardless of the "rules" of the establishment, which often discourage it. One of my particular favourites was a lovely old lady in her nineties, who had been a spiritualist medium in her younger days. She was always cheering me with the messages she had received for me from her spirit guides beyond the veil.

As one of the nurses in charge of the unit my role was mainly supervisory, but I was trained in hands-on nursing and so found my designated approach frustrating. I couldn't resist rolling up my sleeves and getting stuck in. One day, as I walked into Vera's room to massage her legs and give her morning medication, she amused me by saying, "Ah, I knew you were here today, dear." I laughed and said that of course she did; she had seen my little dog. But she insisted that she could "feel" a change in the energy when I was on duty. "No," she told me, "it is because you bring the angels and lots of 'visitors' with you – the angels have just shown me a vision of you riding tandem with a lovely young man. He was at the front pedalling and you were sat on the back, with your feet stretched out to the sides, shouting for him to stop, he was going so fast!"

Shortly after that, single again, I certainly did meet a lovely man on a trip to Australia, and the relationship did go a little too fast for me. Feeling the pressure on his arrival in London, I slammed on the brakes sharply, jumped off and let him pedal away back home!

A gift

Another day when I went in to see her she said, "As you walked through my doorway I saw a huge gift above your head, beautifully wrapped in lovely paper and tied with a big bright-red ribbon. It's from the angels – you have been given a wonderful gift, dear, I know you have a good life ahead of you." I asked her what was in the box, and laughed out loud when she scoffed, "Oh they don't tell me what it is dear… they won't tell me that! It's only for you to know!"

Vera was crippled with painful arthritis. She could only walk from the bedside chair to her bathroom with the support of a frame. Everywhere else, she had to be taken by wheelchair. I had often confided in Vera, talking to her of my research, the angelic synchronicities, the different angels and their guidance. She knew all about my hopes to teach healing work with the angels. One morning I asked her to take part in a little experiment with me, which she happily agreed to do. I explained that I was going to call on archangels and healing angels to help with her pain and asked her to do the same.

A healing channel

So I sat down in front of her on a little footstool and I massaged her legs and knees as I did every shift, but this time I said a prayer. I silently invited the Archangel Raphael to be with me in this exercise and for God to send his angels to help me relieve Vera's pain. I asked that I might be used as a channel for healing energy and that this would flow through me and go wherever it was needed by Vera's body, for however long.

I closed my eyes. The sunlight in the room seemed to turn very bright and I could feel it permeating my body. In a split second I felt a surge of energy run down my arms like electricity. My hands were resting on Vera's knees and they felt very hot. My entire body felt light, as if I was floating, somehow, and I had a sense of complete love – bliss. Within what seemed like just a few moments

I could hear my name being called and knew I must finish the exercise and return to the unit, where someone else needed me.

I thanked God, the angels, grounded myself and opened my eyes. The room was full of sunshine, but there were four green lights dancing around Vera's head. Then, as I looked at Vera, I saw that she had changed. Of course she was still the same old lady, with lines and bent body, but she seemed so beautiful, so calm and so serene. It was very moving.

As Vera opened her eyes she smiled. "That was so beautiful, dear. Did you know that there were two enormous bright angels standing by your sides, with a hand on each shoulder? And around your head there were four tiny winged angels all glowing and dancing in a bright-green light, almost like fairies?" We both cried tears of joy and gratitude. That day Vera walked all the way along the lengthy corridor from her room to the dining room for lunch, with only a frame and one care assistant by her side.

Now, I'm not saying that the event took away Vera's arthritis, or indeed that she was cured of the pain. But something happened that day, for the whole day, and it dramatically changed things for her. Whether the angels had completely removed her pain, or whether it was the power of prayer, or even just her strong faith and firm belief working as "mind over matter", we'll never know, but from that point onward it had a profound impact on my trust in the angels and their ability to heal.

Raphael heals rifts in relationships and mental and emotional issues as well as physical ill health. More and more we are awakening to the understanding of how closely linked emotional issues are to dis-ease in the body, and that working on the spiritual levels will almost definitely help with all types of illness.

Beryl's story

Beryl's story illustrates how the angels can heal the wounds of the heart, which then has a ripple effect throughout our energy bodies (physical, emotional, ethereal and spiritual). Beryl felt that she had never had a good relationship with her father, even at the point of his death. They had not reconciled their differences and several years afterwards Beryl was left with a residue of deep emotional pain.

Tranquillity of nature

She told me that one day, while walking the dog across farmland close to where she lives, she became extraordinarily aware of the peace and tranquillity of the area: the wide expanse of the fields, the trees in the distance, the larks singing high above her head. There was no traffic noise; not even the usual tractor sounds. Beryl felt completely at one with nature and engulfed by peace. Then, suddenly, an overwhelming sense of emotional sadness gripped her and she sobbed and sobbed as though her heart would break. After a few minutes, just as instantly as they had started, the tears stopped. She was aware of a presence of love and a calmness, which replaced all the pain and sorrow related to her relationship with her father. She describes the sensation of love as so great, so healing, so blissful that it was "as though I was surrounded by angels". These were the sensations of angelic healing energy that later, after years of being a medium and training in spiritual healing, Beryl began to recognize as the potent gift of healing energy from the Archangel Raphael.

June's story

A member of my local spiritual development group, June, a woman possessing the warmth that her name might imply, had a wonderful vision of Raphael and the energy of the healing forces. She tells the story for herself:

I had been a healer for many years, then six or seven years ago I began attending meditation sessions. At that time I knew nothing about the angelic world, the archangels, their names or what they represented. Then one afternoon, the group began our second meditation. We were asked to imagine ourselves somewhere we enjoyed being, or in an imaginary place of our choice. My imaginary place was a small cabin, with a garden, on a beach. It is my secret space, where I feel peaceful, safe and spiritual.

We were asked to call upon our angel to step forward into our space and to become visible, for us to feel the presence. Instantly an amazing angel stood before me. He was quite a bit larger than me, with enormous wings down to the ground. As I stood before this angel, he unfolded his wings and wrapped them all around me, encompassing me. It was then that I felt the most overwhelming love. I have never experienced anything like it, nor could I begin to explain the enormity of it. Only others who have experienced it for themselves would understand what I felt.

Still wrapped inside the angel's wings, I began to lift away from the cabin and the two of us rose up and up into the sky. While I continued to receive this overpowering love, we climbed away into the sky and then, after a while, began to return to the cabin.

As the meditation moved to its conclusion, we were to ask our angels if they would give us a name. I received the name and we closed the meditation.

Our group discussed our experience, but I was in floods of tears and could not speak for a while. I was not speechless just because of the amazing meditation experience, but mostly because of the overwhelming love that I had been given. Eventually I was able to tell the group of my time with the angel. "Did you get a name?" they asked. "Yes I was given a most peculiar name," I replied, "it was Raphael."

This was the beginning of my introduction to angels and, as I look back now, I am still awe-struck. I really knew nothing much about them or their identities, so how amazing not only to have this experience, but to have been loved and taken into the sky by Raphael, the Archangel of Healing. What a confirmation of my work as a healer!

June's healing work developed rapidly following this experience and she has since done more work with angelic healing, with great success.

George's story

Over the years I have been so impressed by just how many people have become gifted healers following a profound angelic experience of their own. George is one of my students from Ireland. He is a wonderfully good-humoured and spiritual man, who has also become a healer and believes strongly in the presence of angels. He has recently become a group facilitator and teaches others how to connect with their celestial guardians to receive gifts of healing through meditation.

A turning point

George is convinced that his life was saved in order to work with the angels and be in the service of healing and spiritual discovery. He shyly confessed that he had never shared his story before, but now understands that his journey led him to exactly where he was meant to be. His turning point followed excessive drinking over many years: alcohol addiction had ruined his marriage and it almost destroyed his entire life. He had been brought up in Dublin, with a strict Roman Catholic schooling, and as a young man was very sceptical about the religious life. He described his life-changing experience, which took place when he was in hospital suffering from a punctured oesophagus. He now believes it was a way for the angels to bring him to a place of service.

Out of body

George had cirrhosis of the liver and had been hospitalized following a haemorrhage. The bleeding was halted and as George came round from the anaesthetic he became frighteningly aware that he was "out of his body". He could see his body, which was lying in a bed – the other beds were all hidden by curtains. As he floated above the curtains he saw that a patient at the other end of the long ward was being given morphine and oxygen. A priest was praying over the patient, who, obviously close to death, was receiving the last rites. As George returned to full consciousness, back into his own body, he called the nurse over. "What is going on down there?" he asked her. "Oh nothing, don't you mind, just get some rest now." "No, seriously, I know the man is about to die, there is a priest with him." The nurse looked surprised and left him. The next day, when the same nurse returned, George asked her what the man at the end of the ward had died from. "Cirrhosis of the liver, George, he had a massive haemorrhage. The doctors did their best. He's in a better place now, God willing." George shuddered and resolved to get better.

"Are you interested in angels?" asked the nurse, just before he was discharged from hospital. "Not really." George remembers thinking it a very strange question. The nurse smiled. Her name was Celestine.

Trust in the angels

As if they had been drawn to him by supernatural forces, from that day George kept on meeting people who had experienced angelic or divine intervention that had, in some miraculous way, saved their life. He bought the book *The Celestine Prophecy* and found himself becoming very interested in synchronicity and angels.

The most important lesson working with Raphael has taught me is that, having asked the angels for help and healing, you must believe, because healing occurs in many different ways. You must trust in the outcome. Time after time, as human beings, we doubt our ability to connect with the heavenly realms. We somehow feel too small, too insignificant or unworthy.

We ask for help and rather than asking for the "highest good" or the "best possible outcome for all concerned", we get embroiled in specific subjective, personal and sometimes selfish requests. Then, if the result turns out differently from what we originally requested – even if it is what we actually needed to grow – we can fail to recognize the benefits, doubting that there was any divine guidance, angelic or otherwise.

Yet how much proof do we need?

Lyn's story

This next story is an account of angels from one of my readers. Lyn's deeply held belief and unquestioning faith not only attracted financial abundance just when she needed it, but also helped to heal her partner, enabling him to build confidence and regain dignity.

Often events and incidents are dismissed as chance. As I look back over the years, I would say that this is what I did before I understood, before I first began to wake up and became aware of angels. Our time of redundancies had begun. It seemed everyone over the age of forty was in the frame; employing those with experience and expertise was too expensive when you could get two younger people for the same wage. Sadly my poor partner was made redundant. He took this badly. Becoming acutely depressed, he went to bed for six months, only getting up for one meal a day.

It turned out that the firm he worked for had not paid his National Insurance stamps, and there was no redundancy payment for him. This came as a further shock as he would only receive the very basic amount of financial benefit for his sickness. He felt betrayed and abandoned as he had worked for the firm for nineteen years. My own earnings just about covered household expenses, leaving very little for everyday living. However, I did seem to receive little gifts of help from the angels. On the first occasion my lottery ticket won £90, and with careful management, this extra money lasted for weeks. This was followed by a win of £50 on a Premium Bond from the few we had saved. Again frugal management meant that we kept our dignity.

As each amount ran out and I wondered where I should turn for help, another small amount would arrive from somewhere: never in huge amounts, but enough to meet our needs. This went on for the whole six months, until my partner was better and able to find a job. Interestingly, once he was employed the gifts stopped arriving.

Then suddenly I, too, was made redundant. Aged well over fifty, there seemed no chance of another job. However, this changed within only eight days. I was delighted to find another opportunity and was now employed for double my previous wage.

By this time my interest in spiritual matters had taken me to the local church. It was a great place to sit and contemplate, so tranquil and calm that sometimes I would even drop off to sleep. I became involved in the church and made friends there.

When disaster struck and the roof fell in I was asked if I was any good with money and I half-heartedly agreed to become treasurer of the repair fund. We would need in excess of £20,000. I prayed for assistance and this amount was raised within six months, only to be followed by the need for £10,000 to pay for complete electrical rewiring. This money arrived in the form of interest-free loans.

By this time, I think I was beginning to feel that a greater hand than mine was at work. Although I worked for spiritualists, I didn't feel as though I always fitted in – but I was driven by an honest passion to help. I did not have the gift of mediumship, but I felt drawn toward healing and in time became a qualified healer. It was during training that I first became aware of a great angelic power that is always with us.

Having received such help, Lyn went on to develop astounding healing skills and used her gifts from the angels to make a huge difference in many people's lives.

More and more people are training to become healers. Reiki, Seichem, spiritual healing, Theta, Shefa healing and many other therapeutic techniques are being taught, given and received all over the world. We are becoming more and more aware of the wonderful effect of the gift of healing on ourselves and other people.

Some healers concentrate their gifts by channelling healing energy into places and ancient sites. How does this work?

Sensing events of the past

We now understand that each human cell contains memory: cellular memory held deep within our body, which has been created by a lifetime of thoughts, experiences, fears and joys. Some believe that our cellular memory also contains information from previous lifetimes. Houses, buildings, towns and areas of land also hold the memory of events. Most of us, whether knowingly psychic or not, have entered a place or building where we could feel the energy, or vibration, which we describe as the "atmosphere", often sensing it as very cold. This is particularly common when we are visiting historical sites.

Once, when I was walking in New Zealand, I sat down on a large, flat rock for a rest and, when I closed my eyes, heard loud voices in a language I didn't understand. I felt anger and fear. I was startled, but when I opened my eyes there was no one there except the two friends who had accompanied me to the hills. I closed my eyes to try to recapture the sensation, but the voices had gone. When I described the sounds I had heard, of shouting, clashing and chanting, I was told that we had come to a place of great Maori significance. I was sitting in the heart of a battleground, upon the very stone where Maori chiefs would have cut open the chest of the losing chieftain to remove his heart, thus rendering the tribe powerless.

I felt a bit shaken by that knowledge. I said a prayer and called the Angels of Healing to bring peace to the land, helping to soothe the pain and anger I had felt there. Without realizing, this was one of my first experiences of channelling healing energy to Mother Earth. That gruesome memory took a while to fade.

Some people spend their lives healing areas of land where great battles were fought or atrocities took place. One such group, the Fountain, was formed when community prayer proved to lessen levels of violence in certain towns. The group members decided to meet regularly and go to trouble spots, to pray together and meditate, bringing healing energy to the place. Later studies have shown that the crime rate subsequently fell significantly in those places. Academic studies have been carried out in the USA to show the efficacy of thought and positive energy, and dramatic drops in crime rates have been reported.

Healing wounded places

I moved into the countryside of the Essex–Suffolk border in 2005. Happy to live in such beautiful countryside, I was very surprised at the physical reaction I experienced when driving down the country lanes to and from our village. This is an area of great historical significance and many of the old towns near by are steeped in history and folklore. Thaxted, for example, has a guildhall that dates back to the twelfth century, and the community of our neighbouring village, Finchingfield, where the guildhall still stands, is mentioned in the Doomsday Book (completed in 1086). We are also close to the route to Colchester, Britain's oldest town, and significantly near to the stretch of land where Boudicca led her warriors in revenge against the Romans, who had raped her daughters.

Physical pain

I felt an actual pain in my chest and an awareness of being watched as I drove home, particularly in the early evenings. I often arrived home exhausted, but I didn't know why. I have always enjoyed driving and did not think that country roads should be any more stressful than driving in congested cities.

I decided to make some enquiries. As I drove my mother through the same lanes on one of her visits, I asked her if she picked up on any strange energy. At first she was just delighted by the scenery, until we reached the lanes that troubled me to my core. I had not mentioned which area bothered me in particular, but the moment we started driving down my "troublesome" road she whispered, "It's right here!" She too could feel such sadness and pain held in the ether. As soon as we were closer to home she told me that the feelings had gone.

It began to distress me and when I tried to describe to my husband how I felt, I could only tell him that it was as though the lanes were lined with dead people, and although I could only sense them fleetingly, they could all see me. In my mind's eye there were many of them, yet not all of them were from the distant past. Some were young, some old, some wounded, some in rags and some in modern dress; many of them were soldiers from various wars and several were young motorcyclists.

My mother and I sat together and called upon God's Angels of Light to bring peace to the many souls. We called to Archangel Raphael, the Angel of Consecration, to bring solace to the whole area and soothe the earth and her memories, healing the pain she held in the energy of that area of land.

Where we are most needed

Later, on a visit to Ireland, I was staying with another angel worker, the clairvoyant healer and angel therapist, Aidan Storey. He and I were conducting a series of workshops and I described my concerns about my new location. He turned to me with a look of disbelief. "I can't believe that you seriously don't know what it is you are doing there!" he said.

We laughed together as slowly the penny dropped. I related the story of my sense of urgency to get away from London and move into the country, of being drawn to the small village of Wethersfield, 50 miles away, of falling in love with our little house and moving there, even though it wasn't where we actually wanted to live and I missed London badly. He went on to explain his theory: "Some of us have agreed to work as 'gateways' to the many souls who are wandering, painfully lost, trapped by their trauma, and who do not know how to get back to the Light. Chrissie, they are drawn to the light created by your work with the angels, they see this light as you are passing by. You have agreed at a soul level to be a guiding light, which doesn't only mean through your teaching. They see you and return through you into the Light itself. That is what the pain in your chest represents. We are called to where we are most needed. Don't worry, this is only a practice run; you have bigger tasks ahead!"

"Great," thought I!

As many seasons have passed the pain has eased in my chest and the lanes are more comfortable to drive through. Now, five years on, I hardly notice anything at all. Whether that means my work is complete here I don't know, but I certainly have a yearning now to move on again. Perhaps my work with the angels is taking me somewhere else.

A place in need of healing

When my partner, Brian, and I got married in 2009 we did not really plan a honeymoon, but decided that we would visit one of the places on our wish-list the following winter, to escape from the dreary cold weather. As I was too busy for lengthy research I left the decision entirely to my husband. Knowing that he wanted to visit New Zealand, land of the making of *The Lord of the Rings*, or maybe the Holy Land, or even Australia to visit cousins, I was quite shocked when he suddenly announced he had found a super deal on a holiday to the Dominican Republic. A Caribbean holiday to jazzy Cuba, perhaps – but neither of us had ever mentioned the Dominican Republic before. Nevertheless we discussed it, booked and, after further deliberation, paid.

Puzzled and a tiny bit disappointed at the destination, I wondered about our choice, but having relinquished my half of the decision I could hardly complain. In any case that would have seemed dreadfully ungracious. After all, we were heading off to sunshine, palm trees and white beaches and I did have a pile of books waiting to be read.

The next morning we came down to the news that Haiti had experienced its worst earthquake ever. "You do realize this is the same island?" Brian asked me as we watched the news in horror. I was deeply affected by the devastation; we both were. Then he suggested we should cancel our trip immediately. Morally, he felt that we couldn't possibly enjoy ourselves in luxury when people on the other side of the island had lost their homes and even their lives.

As the day passed and we watched more bulletins, it became clear that we would go. I knew we were meant to be there. Trying to lift my spirits, Brian joked, "Well I'm not making a decision again, if that's what happens when I press the 'pay now' button!". But my mind was already racing to the prospect of gathering like-minded friends and students to send out prayers, healing energy and light to the affected area. Intuitively I knew that it was no coincidence, and that somehow I was part of a divine plan. The angelic realms had arranged for me to be there to be used as an anchor of light. I would, after five years of practice helping to release souls in my own country, be able to offer my service, in some small way, to those who might be trapped in negativity, in the depths of despair and fear. I was called to deep prayer, and I knew what I had to do.

By pure coincidence, my colleague, Richard, had been urging me to create better contact lists and now I had an even clearer reason for building a large database. I wrote to all my contacts asking for help – to all the groups of students, to my Essene friends and to networks of healers all over the world.

Anchor of healing

I also enlisted the help of the two spiritual development groups that I held locally, on Tuesdays and Thursdays. We all agreed that they would light a candle at the usual group-meeting time and sit together in meditation, sending healing energy through me to the island. I would receive their energy to strengthen me while I was being used as a conduit of healing energy far away in the Dominican Republic.

As each day dawned during my two weeks away, I started with the Essene communions, calling in the Angels of the Earthly Mother and the Angels of the

Heavenly Father. In my meditation I became taller and stronger, visualizing the light running through me into the ground. At midday I called upon the spiritual healing of the angels to fill those working in Haiti with energy and life force. Mid-afternoon, I linked for half an hour in meditation with all the groups, as arranged by email, for them to send concentrated healing energy through me, as an anchor to the island.

On each Tuesday and Thursday, I visualized all the members of my own groups standing in a circle and sending me their love and healing light. Of course millions of prayers were being sent at the same time from people all over the world who had nothing to do with me, but my own prayers and guidance led me to take this particular action.

In the evenings, for the two weeks, I stood on our balcony and prayed for the souls in torment to be released into God's love, and visualized the angels escorting them lovingly into the heavenly bright light of safety and peace. My husband knew I was doing something extra, as I was rather quiet at certain times of the day. He remains fairly sceptical of my work, and so much of the time I tend to simply "get on with it" in my own way. The afternoon meditations were easy as most people were sleeping after lunch. I now realize that they would anyway have been consumed with their own thoughts and not terribly interested in the meditative practices of a rather eccentric middle-aged woman on the beach!

At many other times, too, I was able to slip into a meditative sacred space, or I would walk along the beach, asking that the energy of peace and calm, healing and love be carried through me and down from my feet into the water washing round to Haiti, beyond the mountain range and just around the bay.

Orbs of energy

On the last night of our stay, after a day of heavy rain, I was standing on our balcony watching the drops falling gracefully from a palm outside our window. This is so beautiful, I thought, like a scene from *Fantasia*. There was a strange calmness, yet it was infused with a life force that felt electric. I must take a photograph, I thought. I took three, one after the other, aiming at the palm tree through the darkness, and again into the deep-black, rain-filled Caribbean evening sky. Brian came out, so I took a picture of him, too.

I looked back through the digital images to see if I had captured the beauty of the scene. To my astonishment each of the photographs was covered in orbs of light. Raindrops were there, too, but the orbs were in a swirling pattern, some large, some small, but all bright and full of light. Among the white orbs, some orbs had colour. Then, as if to prove that they are not always visible, particularly to the non-believer, the photograph I had taken of Brian contained only droplets of pure rain. I stared at the pictures. It was impossible not to be moved by them. It was just as though the orbs of spiritual energy had come to say farewell.

Reporting back

My adventure had not ended there as I was yet to hear, on my return, all the amazing stories of the visions seen in meditation and the other experiences that had taken place in the groups while I was away. One lady reported that some in her group had seen the faces of women and children being escorted by angels. My ladies' group had held special prayers and sent me healing to give me strength on Thursday night. That afternoon I had a vision of six of them sitting in a circle. I connected with each in turn and felt the energy and love from every woman. One of the ladies saw me standing at the edge of the ocean with my feet in the water and my face raised to the sun. She called upon Raphael, who guided healing through me into the water, and she told me that she then saw a beam of sunlight pointing toward my head and from my feet into the sea.

Maggie's story

The most remarkable story was that of Maggie, my group organizer, driver and close companion in Belfast.

Maggie had also agreed to connect with me at specific times of day. On the same day as the Dunmow group had been experiencing such a strong connection, she had been sitting in her healing room dedicating the same time to link in to me. Maggie's room is a sanctuary of angels. She has books, oils, pictures, cards, candles and crystals all dedicated to her work with the angels.

She had no way of knowing where I was or what I was doing; only that this was the time we had agreed. First she said some prayers, then she invoked the presence of the angels and connected with them in meditation. As Maggie sat in meditation, sending me light, she felt a strong angelic presence. The angel told her that she was from the moon and was going to take Maggie on a journey. She held Maggie as they flew together straight into the light of the moon. There they seemed to gain energy and Maggie felt very strong and empowered.

Then the moon angel took Maggie to Haiti. As they flew through the ether she saw the outline of the island. They flew over the beaches of the Dominican Republic and Maggie could see me standing at the edge of the water. They flew through the mountains and came to land on the broken ground of Haiti. She could feel the sorrow in every cell of her body and almost taste the fear in the air. She could feel the heaviness of destruction, death and despair.

Heart connection

Then, streaming over Maggie and the moon angel, came a powerful beam of light. It spread golden light everywhere they went. They lifted off the ground together and flew slowly back toward the Dominican Republic. They prayed in unison and Maggie could feel her heart connect to the heart energy of the souls trapped in Haiti. As they passed, the souls were released into the Light, and as the night drew forward the cracks in the land began to heal. When dawn began to bring sunlight to the island, Maggie sensed that earth was being bathed by divine light, forgiveness and loving healing.

The angel brought Maggie to my side as I was standing with my feet in the sea. She gave me a hug of intense healing energy and love, and witnessed the flow of light through my body into the sand and out with the gentle waves into the sea. After her powerful and intense meditation experience, Maggie contemplated her role in the visualization and wondered at the ability we have to release souls into the Light. The next day she received a book written by a friend, which her husband had ordered for her. As she opened the book, the dedication printed inside sent a tingle through her body. It said, "Dedicated with love to the real moon fairy".

Meditation for Healing

Whether you choose to be outdoors in the fresh air or find a place inside where you can be alone to listen to soft music and light a candle, please switch off your mobile phone and dedicate these few minutes to your own healing process. You deserve it.

The idea is to practise sitting quietly so that you can visualize a beautiful, calm scene of green fields, meadows, trees and grassy lawns; a scene of tranquillity that will bring you balance – emotionally, mentally, spiritually and physically.

- Breathe slowly and deeply, filling your abdomen as well as your lungs. Count at least ten in-breaths before proceeding, and with every exhalation relax the muscles of your body.
- See yourself surrounded by a mist of green healing light encircling your body from crown to feet and say to yourself three times, "Every cell in my being works in perfect harmony."
- Allowing the green light to permeate your body, imagine that all tensions, aches and pains and emotional turmoil is being soothed and healed. Trust

that the angels are with you. Thank them and yourself for taking part in the meditation.

"I am transformed and healed as I recognize my interconnection with the healing power of the Divine."

CHAPTER 4

GIFTS OF GUIDANCE AND WISDOM

Knowledge can be gained from many sources, but wisdom is a quality that arises from within. Wisdom involves a greater understanding of the wider picture; Archangel Gabriel and the angels urge us to develop an inner wisdom that reflects a broader view of the whole experience of life.

We are often raised by our parents to be independent and self-sufficient – a good thing in itself – but the angelic bigger picture shows us that once we have opened our hearts to compassion and wisdom we no longer exist as a single unit, but rather as a part of the interconnected everything that is.

This is how we are able to learn to sense the angels when they are close to us. We sometimes feel their presence, hear their whispers, sense the vibrancy of their light surrounding us or simply act differently on impulse. All these are gifts of wisdom that the angels bring to guide us.

"Sometimes what we believe as coincidence is really just getting ourselves caught in an angel booby trap."

GREY LIVINGSTON

We probably would agree that we have a soul purpose. Whether we know and fully understand what that is, or are busy seeking it, our soul resonates to the particular vibrational quality – a unique frequency – of each of the angels working on that same path of service. Our aim is to finely tune and raise our distinct vibration so that it is in tune with that of the angels.

So how do we raise that vibration? How do we know what to do? If our vibration is too dense, too low, then we may in any case be unaware of the spiritual aspects of life. People with a very low vibration are often insensitive to the needs of others and not yet familiar with the spiritual. Those who are in this state of being are often referred to as not yet "awake". Once we are awake the hard work starts! What do we do then?

Awakening is like a flag that suddenly shoots from your crown, a beam of light that proclaims to the universe, "Hey, celebrate with me, I'm back… I remembered!" The heavenly realms rejoice and your team of angels is immediately by your side, pulling together the right circumstances, people and teachers, books and courses for your rapid development. Yes, you probably know exactly how it all works. Negative people, places, feelings about the self and others, and toxic substances all gradually fade as the heart becomes more open, allowing our wisdom and compassion space to grow. This is what raises our vibration.

We live in an extraordinary era. For the first time in history everything we want to know about spiritual beliefs and cultures, the religions and rituals from all over the world is readily available at our fingertips. Thanks to easy access to information, more and more of us are waking up. Many wonderful beings, often referred to as "old souls", have incarnated into this lifetime in order to carry out a high level of service to humanity, which at a soul level they have agreed to fulfil. Sometimes they don't actually remember what it is; in other cases a situation, a coincidence or a serendipitous meeting will trigger the memory.

Kate's story

Kate, an American, was just passing the building of the Theosophical Society in London, coincidentally on the day I was there giving a talk about connecting with angels. Noticing people gathering in groups outside, she was curious to find out what was going on. She came inside to see if she would feel drawn to join in.

Having had an experience once in her life of the wisdom and guidance of her guardian angel, she decided to attend my talk and join the group meditation and sharing. She was impressed and moved by the ease with which, during a guided visualization, she found herself deepening her connection with the archangels. She seemed a confident, knowledgeable lady when she approached me at the end of my talk. Her eyes and demeanour told me that she was indeed a very old soul. Kate said that an angel had visited her in her youth and given her much-needed reassurance about the future.

When I was fifteen I was full of despair. I thought that nothing in the world would ever go right for me. I was extremely depressed and in a bad, dark place. Suddenly I felt the presence of "someone" talking to me, yet there was no one around. I was told that all would be well; there was no need to fear and that I would pass all my exams and go on to high school (college). I was given detailed information about certain aspects of my life that were causing me huge anxiety. The angel messenger told me that I would soon forget what I was being told, but that by the time I was twenty-one everything would be fine, and that as an adult, I would remember what I had been told and what had come to pass. Now, in my fifties, I look back and understand that this was my guardian angel reassuring me and foretelling my future. Although I do not have much intellectual knowledge of angels I have been immensely grateful for that visitation of guidance.

When we feel drawn to working with angels, at whatever level is comfortable for us, and our energetic vibration is heightened, we are more able to perceive the angels in some form. This very often follows a significant vision, a dream, an encounter or a healing during which a shift occurs that cannot be explained. We have come to know these as angelic experiences because as human beings it is normal for us to categorize, but "angel" simply means messenger, and a messenger of God may take many guises.

Test of faith?

After I had completed a course in angelic healing with angel artist Jayne in north London, Jayne asked me to co-present workshops with her. She felt our energies were complementary, since she had years of experience but was very quietly spoken and sensitive, and I was more extrovert and openly enthusiastic. We ran successful events called "angel days" in east London, in which we invited other therapists and spiritual teachers to take part. We also co-facilitated workshops in London and Sheffield. We worked together wherever Jayne was guided by her angels, and soon I started doing the work on my own.

I was invited to appear in a special feature called *I Believe in Angels* on the television chat show presented by Robert Kilroy-Silk. The feature was investigating the existence of angels. It was an audience-participation programme and I had been pre-warned that I would be asked to tell my story and answer questions, along with other invited "believers", and also that I should prepare myself for debate, as there would be a number of invited "non-believers" to liven up the show.

Preparation and apprehension

I was up early, sat in meditation and called upon the angels for guidance. I was conscious of a growing sense of responsibility, mixed with apprehension at the thought of appearing on television for the first time. To help me relax and connect with nature, I decided to take my little dog for a walk. As I collected my post on the way, I found to my horror a strangely worded letter from Jayne, my "spiritual" teacher, whom I had trusted as a friend, terminating our working relationship and our friendship. I was so upset by the letter. The words jumped from the paper into my mind, where they rippled in ever-increasing circles, "shouting" in my ears. I felt nauseous. I was horrified to think that I had caused offence, and shocked that she seemed so jealous of my new life. She had clearly timed the letter to arrive just before the TV filming. I wasn't sure whether I would be capable of going ahead with the programme after all.

Tearfully, I walked to the park, confused and hurting from the unexpected rejection. Embarrassed by my tears, I hid inside the long, trailing branches of a huge old willow tree. I called upon the angels to help me find inner calm, to take away the pain and heal the wound caused by my reaction to the letter. As usual in difficult situations I found myself talking to God and then calling upon Archangel Raphael, the great wise healer. I implored Gabriel to light the way forward, Michael to help me release my attachment, Uriel to strengthen my resolve and give me inner peace, and Chamuel to raise my self-esteem with love.

My prayers answered

As I leant against the trunk of my sturdy new friend the willow tree, with its majestic height and glorious trailing branches, I felt an immediate calmness, an inner strength and a feeling of reverence. Within an instant, the angels had answered my call. All previously painful thoughts melted away, taking away any attachment to the thought of the letter or the behaviour behind it. I found myself distracted by the incredible brightness and beauty of the sunlight playing on the water of the canal. It was as though I was standing inside a natural cathedral. The peace and tranquillity within the walls of leaves made it a sacred space and I felt alive, invigorated and loved. I was so overtaken by the blissful sense of joy that, as I left the tree, thanking it for its sanctuary, I almost forgot my patient little dog sitting at the base of the great trunk waiting for me.

I strolled back to my apartment with a new lightness. The car duly arrived to take me to the studio. The session turned into a lively audience debate, in which many of us shared amazing angelic experiences. For me, great friendships and connections were made which were to prove invaluable over the next few years. I don't know why Jayne sent me the letter, but I have often reflected that perhaps it was a test of faith. Asking the angels for help and guidance doesn't just work – it works instantly!

Pete's story

Stepping up, "raising our vibration", requires us to develop new personal and spiritual skills, emotionally, physically and intellectually. The lessons in discernment that we are given are sometimes confusing and difficult. But however hard the lessons seem, we are always given the means to handle them. This is when wisdom begins to grow: not from books or intellectual learning, but from developing compassion, empathy and discernment. Pete's connection to the angels illustrates this perfectly, demonstrating how angelic guidance leaves him with new understanding.

For years now I have sensed the angels talking to me. They have helped with my relationships and my life in general. Although I cannot see anything, I feel a presence and they communicate with me by whispering.

I sense that over the years these heavenly messengers, my angels, have moved up through some kind of celestial hierarchy – because, just as I think I am getting things right, they give me messages that indicate I need to "step up" and raise my standards. As they move higher they seem to want me to do the same. They seem to be guiding me upward. Looking back, I know they have helped me enormously.

Pete's words also show that each of us has a unique way of communicating with the angels, depending on our own skills and preferences. Wisdom and encouragement in the form of spiritual guidance come to us in different ways. We do not all see or feel things around us. For some, such as Pete, the angels and guides release their messages deep into the inner ear, where they are heard as a "whispering". The recipient feels the message internally, as a sense of knowing.

Angelic guidance and wisdom don't always change your life instantly, and can be related to future events. Even if the meaning doesn't become obvious until much later, the presence of angels is always reassuring.

Stan's story

Another case of an unexplained happening was sent to me by Stan Garrett, a Reiki master and psychic healer, who has been working with spiritual energies for many years. In this encounter the guidance was undoubtedly supernatural. Rather than being a subtle whisper, it was a bright light that guided him physically out of a dense, dark wood.

It is winter, December 1955. I have just left Wendover railway station at 12.30am. I walk along the road that leads back to the Halton Royal Air Force camp, where I'm currently stationed. It's cold and very black, no moon, nor any stars. I can hardly find my way along the road, but my eyes are becoming accustomed to what little light there is and I can see faint outlines of hedgerows, the pavement and the road ahead.

I haven't got a pass, so I have to dodge the guardroom by turning off the road and making my way through a wood. I know that the visibility will worsen once I enter the trees. I struggle to make out a pathway as I leave the road. Then, in front of me, is the track that leads through the wood. As I look ahead I can see how it enters the wood and then disappears into complete blackness.

I enter the wood and the darkness closes in. Feeling that I'll have to turn back, I decide to ask for help from Spirit. Suddenly, at the other end of the track, is a white light that allows me to see my way. Could it be from the guardroom? I'm past caring. Over the next few minutes I trudge through the wood, guided by the light. Now it is directly in front of me, about 2ft away, the size of a football and hovering at chest level. I'm tempted to reach out and touch it, but instead I just stand there and watch and wait. After a few minutes, which seem like hours, it suddenly moves off, zigzagging through the trees at tremendous speed, before disappearing out of sight.

Whatever it was, the light enabled me to navigate through the wood. On reflecting on this incident, with another fifty-odd years of experience with the paranormal, I can only conclude that I was guided by angels or by my guardian angel.

A story about Gabriel

Sometimes guidance comes along in a different light form, as a group of us found, to our great amusement, at the end of a workshop in the Midlands. The organizer, June, and I were sitting processing the day's events before my long drive south when the telephone rang. It was June's mother and I could hear that she was in tears. She had been at the workshop that day and had very much enjoyed the meditation that takes participants on a journey to meet their guardian angel, so I was concerned in case her experience had troubled her.

During the question-and-answer session at the end of the workshop, this lovely lady had revealed to the group that the angel had given the name Gabriel. For whatever reason she persuaded herself that this simply was not possible and that the angel Gabriel could not, under any circumstances, be her guardian angel. After all, was that not the archangel who had brought news to Mary in the Bible? She believed, as she left that day's workshop, that this was far too grand an angel for the likes of such an "ordinary woman". We teased her a little by suggesting that perhaps even Mary at the time thought of herself as just an "ordinary woman".

A sign

Then, on her journey home, came a turn of events that shook her to the core. She was pondering on her guardian angel, the name and the gift she had been given. Up until that point she had never doubted the presence of angels in her life and had simply come along to the workshop to re-affirm this and share experiences with other like-minded souls in a safe space. But the name, this name, had been a little much for her. So she closed her eyes for a couple of moments and said a little prayer. "Please give me your name again," she asked quietly, "and this time let me know for sure."

I had instructed my group – as I always do – to ask for signs from the angels in a way that is unique, so that you cannot mistake it.

As her bus left the terminus a white van pulled in front, taking its place in the traffic queue. She was sitting at the front of the bus and the van travelled right in front of her window, where it remained for the whole journey home. Across the doors was written "GABRIEL at your service".

We have been given the impression that as human beings we are hierarchically "below" the angels, that God has created us inferior by creating us mortal. We may find it hard to believe that an angel, let alone an archangel, would ever grace us with his presence. This is not true. But it does tell us much about our own self-esteem and our lack of confidence in our own spirituality.

Bringing order

By 1999 my angel work was increasing, and it was then that I, too, had an experience of the effect of talking to Archangel Gabriel. I had recently started up a series of "angel parties". I would be invited to go along to someone's home with my books and saleable angel items and we would have a chat about angels – biblical angels, angels from other religions and how to contact our own guardian angels. I would lead a guided visualization for participants to meet their angel and receive a symbolic spiritual gift, which we would then discuss, as well as sharing our angel experiences.

It was a wonderful time, but because I was working full-time, my admin was getting a little out of control. So I asked Archangel Gabriel to help me. In my evening meditational prayers I asked if I could please have some help – as Gabriel's task was to bring divine order to the world – in bringing order to my life.

A helping hand

The next day I was busy on a late shift handing out medication to the residents when one of the relatives came to talk to me. I had often seen him visiting his mother, one of my favourite old ladies, and so was happy to stop to give him my attention. "I just wanted to thank you from the bottom of my heart," he said. "Do you realize that it's such a relief to our family that mum feels so safe in the home and that you help to make her stay here a happy one? So I just wanted to say that if there is ever anything I can do to help you in return, all you have to do is ask."

"Well that's so kind of you," I said. "I'm actually just enjoying doing my job, but I am very fond of your mother, so that makes it easy work." Then, quite out of the blue, and quite out of character, as I'm not good at asking direct questions, I turned and asked him, "What is it you do?"

"I'm a chartered accountant," he replied. "Any time you need some help with your tax returns just give me a call."

"Whoa, that was quick!" I exclaimed. "Thank you, Gabriel!" I quickly explained how I had asked for help from the Archangel Gabriel. "Ah that would explain your affinity with my mother," he said. "She is strong in her Jewish faith and believes in the angels." He gave me his card and generously helped me to organize my affairs by completing my annual tax return for the next couple of years.

While some people are confidently able to talk with angels, others may feel their presence and guidance intuitively, without even realizing it. Angels don't always make their appearance felt in loud thunderclaps and flashes of light. More often it goes unnoticed, in what may seem to be small, everyday occurrences.

The runaway boy

Here is a story about a young boy's need of angelic guidance. He may, or may not, have been aware of his angels, but I believe that they were certainly guiding him.

One day the doorbell rang while I was involved in a lengthy phone discussion. My husband came to find me, indicating that I should get off the phone. Excusing myself, I went to the door. There stood a small boy, head stooped, holding his coat in his hands. Brian looked at me and shrugged questioningly. "He says he has run away," he quietly whispered.

I crouched down to the boy's level and gently asked him his name and how I could help him. "I'm Paul. I've run away," he told me in a timid voice. "They won't listen, and it's not fair." I pondered what to do first.

"Where do you live, Paul?" I asked him. "Braintree," he said. Braintree was about 7 miles away. "And you walked all this way, through the country lanes? What time did you leave home?" "About half past eleven."

He had been walking for four and a half hours. "I'll bet you're thirsty and hungry, aren't you?" I said. "OK. Come on in and we'll try to sort this out and get you home again."

"I like your angel," he said, pointing to the huge tapestry of an angel playing a flute that was hanging on the staircase wall. Brian and I exchanged glances; I knew the angels had brought him here.

A crystal child

Paul told me that he was twelve, though he seemed slight for his age. He held his head down most of the time, but when I finally got a clear look into his beautiful face I was overwhelmed by a momentary recognition as I saw his large, deep-blue eyes and long eyelashes. I was so touched by the openness of his face, knowing intuitively that he was one of the super-sensitive, very special "crystal children". Many of these children have incarnated recently, bringing great wisdom and understanding. They are usually psychic and their high sensitivity makes ordinary life hard for them. They are often misunderstood, misdiagnosed and labelled with a psychological disorder. Some of their spiritual and psychic abilities can be dampened by lack of encouragement and also by food additives and prescription drugs.

Paul looked very sad, so to make him smile I told him a story about how my son, Dan, ran away when he was six. He had taken his pyjamas, a toothbrush and his teddy bear, leaving me a note saying he had "gon forevar", but then came home again, as expected, for his tea. After three huge slices of fruitcake and a whole carton of apple juice, Paul started to tell me why he felt he had to run away. I felt a pang of pain for him, but also huge empathy for his worried family. It turned out that he had no mum, but a young brother of five and an older sister of thirteen. He had suddenly left his family while they were out shopping because he felt he was being blamed unfairly for something by his poor nan, who had been looking after all three children.

He couldn't remember his full address or home phone number. I knew his family would be distraught. And so, at his own suggestion (because he had run away once before), we phoned the police. They had been searching for him since the morning and had even dispatched helicopters. They told us that he had a diagnosis of autism and they had feared for his safety.

Safe passage

The road Paul had walked along is extremely dangerous and notorious for traffic accidents. Although seemingly quiet and picturesque it can be very busy with speeding motorbikes and heavy farm vehicles. There are no pavements or even grass verges, and because of the many twists and turns some of the bends are blind to oncoming traffic. Trees and hedgerows hang over, disguising ditches in many places, and to avoid brambles and stinging nettles he would have had to walk on the road itself for several miles.

Ours is an unassuming red-brick house, lying almost at the back of the village and right at the end of a row of sixteenth-century cottages. I asked Paul if he knew why he had turned into our little lane, which isn't on a route through the village, and finally knocked at our door. I wondered why he had walked through two other villages and yet not stopped to ask anyone else for help. He smiled and shrugged. Then after a few moments he told me, "I just didn't want to stop until I got here. I can't explain. I liked the white door, it felt right, so I rang the bell."

As he left I gave him a hug and he thanked me. Then, as he walked past the staircase, he turned and looked at the wall-hanging of the angel. "I *do* like that angel," he repeated. I silently surrounded him in light, asking the angels to go with him.

And that is how angels work. A vulnerable, sensitive child was protected and guided along a very dangerous stretch of busy, twisting country road. The angels took him to safety. On a normal Saturday most people are out and about. Angels brought Paul to a "safe house" – and we were in. How intriguing. What a privilege. This is why many are drawn to angels and become light workers: so that they may be guided by angels to be in the right place at the right time and continue to do the angels' work, on the ground.

Who knows why we are drawn through certain doors. How many times do we experience a coincidence, which leads us to a situation or encounter that gives us a powerful moment of healing, guidance or wisdom? Sometimes great wisdom comes from a chance encounter, which retrospectively may be seen as divine coincidence.

Jane's story

Another angel-workshop facilitator, Jane Circle, wrote to me about her particular gift from the angels.

There are many times when I feel real angel guidance, but there is one story, in particular, which I always come back to as it had such a profound effect on me. It was in March 2009 that I held my first angel workshop. Afterwards, I picked up the kids from my mum's and headed for home. As I was passing through my local town I felt an angelic guide telling me to go into a shop. The shop was an interior design shop and I always liked visiting it. On this particular day I had no plans to call in, but I decided to heed the guidance (the angels haven't let me down yet!) and went in with my son (aged four) and daughter (aged seven).

We found there were already two ladies in the shop. The owner of the shop had a small, very friendly dog and the children went over, as usual, to pet her. I still had no idea what I was doing there and no clue why the angels would have guided me in. Then one of the ladies started chatting to my kids. I could see that she seemed kind and friendly, so I didn't interrupt. After a while she asked their names. When my son told her that his name was Conrad, she looked shocked. I mumbled that it was an unusual name but she said no, that wasn't why she was surprised – it was because Conrad had been the name of her godfather. Sensing what was going on, I asked for her godfather's surname. She told me his name was Wells.

I was instantly overwhelmed with emotion as I knew this lady must be the goddaughter of my beloved dad, who had passed away in 1979, when I was nine years old. I took a moment to calm my tears and then told her that the little boy was her godfather's grandson.

This lady was a complete stranger to me, but we spent wonderful minutes sharing memories and tears at this unlikely meeting. I then knew why I'd had to go into the shop. The angel guides really do never let me down!

Meditation for Wisdom

One of the most beautiful ways of connecting with the angels, in order to develop your inner wisdom and ability to trust the guidance that you are receiving, is to practise a regular form of angel meditation.

You may already be meditating regularly, or have favourite prayers that you enjoy using to connect with God and the angels, but here is a guided visualization that you might also like to try.

- First, find a warm, quiet place, with no phones to distract you. Light a candle, if possible, with the intention of bringing in the angelic light. You might like to play some peaceful, soothing music.
- Sit comfortably in a relaxed upright position and breathe deeply, slowly filling your abdomen as well as your lungs.
- Imagine roots from your feet going into the ground, anchoring you, as you continue to breathe deeply.
- Now open your crown, visualizing bright white light connecting you to the source of all love and wisdom. Bring the light through your body and, with every in-breath, relax all your muscles and allow the light to flow through you.
- Choose your favourite colour and imagine it as a bright, swirling mist surrounding you.
- Call your angels, or one of the archangels, to come close to you now. If you have been troubled by an

issue, ask for the angel associated with that situation to come forward to guide you. Whatever it is you would like guidance with, visualize the situation in your mind's eye, seeing the preferred outcome – the best solution for all concerned.

- Observe other senses, sensations or sounds, noting any physical changes in your body and your emotions. Take your time. Without trying too hard, ask for signs that will become clear to you afterwards, later in the day or week.
- Thanking the angels for their assistance, from your heart, whatever the outcome may be, breathe yourself back into the moment.

As you extinguish the candle send the angelic light with love to where it is most needed.

"I connect with universal angelic wisdom as
I learn to trust my inner knowing."

CHAPTER 5

GIFTS OF CREATIVITY

The beauty of creation surrounds us. With every breath we breathe, every word spoken, every gesture and action taken we are part of the continually changing universe. The Archangel Jophiel and the Angels of Illumination work closely with great dedication to enable us to see the beauty and creativity in all things. Once we learn to allow creative energy to flow through us, we are enabled to harness divine inspiration and dynamism to channel our positive energies toward co-creation itself.

"When we see through the eyes of an angel, the light and beauty of the universe is reflected back to us."

Although we tend to associate creativity with the arts, such as painting, writing or music, the creativity to which I am referring in this chapter is not just of the "arty" type. It is about how we form the world we live in – our lives and our experiences. Everything we think, say or do creates our life story, which is the story we tell to others and the story we tell to ourselves. We continually create and re-create our own world. Wherever we are in this emerging story, it is profoundly helpful to our spiritual development and self-understanding to review the narrative from time to time. We need to see how we have adapted along the way to the influences upon us. Also, as we view our progress through life, we may simplify, complicate or entirely change our story. We can and may. The choice is ours.

Every form of life has its own essence and a story to tell. From rocks, trees, mountains and stars to rivers, oceans, animals and plants, there is an interconnectedness that becomes part of our human experience as soon as we open or awaken to our own spirituality. The angels are here to help us understand that interconnectedness.

In some of the stories you are about to read, you might recognize certain themes of your own. The stories may stimulate memories that enrich your reflection on aspects of your own life story. From sensations of the visible and tangible, to the invisible and ethereal, all are part of the oneness and beauty of creation.

The visible world, not just your own life, is constantly changing. We are slowly beginning to grasp the idea that as individuals we don't just create our own reality but, together with our fellow human beings, co-create our entire world. But what does it actually mean when we say that we are co-creating our reality?

Energy follows thought

You may already be familiar with the idea that "energy follows thought". Thoughts create the words and ideas, which, when enhanced with emotion, build energy. As we express these words/ideas/emotions we build a scene that can add or detract from our everyday experience. Each scenario created by our personal expression is not only seen through our own eyes, but also affects how everyone around us experiences that moment, too. We all know how it feels to walk into a room where a heated discussion has just taken place, even when the combatants have stopped arguing.

As individuals and collectively, we have thoughts, words and actions that create such powerful energy that when they are combined with other spiritual and natural forces (including our guides, angels and God) we actually manifest that which we believe to be true. What we see and experience as real life around us becomes "reality".

For example, if we believe that everything turns out to be disappointing and negative we will not only have great difficulty feeling blessed, but may actually create an unhappy life, by always feeling disillusioned and deprived. If we look for positives in every outcome we will generally feel happy and be in the fortunate position of automatically counting our blessings.

Once we begin to appreciate fully how this works, we can take responsibility for the words, actions and experiences that we produce. Acting responsibly actually means responding sensibly. At first, like an orchestra of many different instruments learning to play together, it may feel strange, but with practice we will all start playing in tune. Thus a beautiful harmony will evolve, creating a sense of unity and peace in our world.

As above, so below

By the universal law of "As above, so below", it is believed that angels and ancestral spirit guides are working with us all the time to create a harmonious and peaceful world. They have been part of our co-creation since the beginning of time.

The ancient Jewish and Zoroastrian cosmology, found in ancient scriptures, tells of how great angels were created first in order to assist in the manifestation of the universe. As spiritual representations of the Divine Mind, of God, they each became responsible for a particular aspect of that creation. My belief is that these angels are working through many of us now, bringing divine spiritual gifts via a renewed connection to the great archangels. These gifts are shared generously with us in the hope of bringing compassion, beauty, guidance, protection, love and joy into our everyday perception.

The urgent messages coming from the angels, during this time of great change, are all of the pressing need for recognition of interconnectedness. Their hope is that by sharing their gifts we will remember our connection, our role as preservers, our responsibility as custodians of this beautiful planet that is our home while we experience our soul's journey through time itself.

Sometimes spiritual gifts can be expressed in ways that may seem a little obscure. But I'm sure you will agree that many of our deepest and most treasured moments in life are often difficult to express in words; they are what we call "ineffable".

Let me start by sharing some of the stories from my friends who are also spiritual teachers, as they relate their experiences of connection between the angelic realms and us here. They tell of creative gifts that have encouraged, mystified and motivated them in the co-creation of great beauty, inspirational paintings, songs and music, and spiritual teachings.

Theolyn's story

First is a personal story from Theolyn Cortens, founder of Soul School. We have co-facilitated workshops on occasion, and have shared similar spiritual ideals and experiences in our teaching.

Over thirty years ago I had an awe-inspiring experience that was to change my life. I was lying ill in bed, meditating, when I heard sweet voices telling me I would meet my God. I immediately wondered if I was going to die – though I only had mumps! I had no sense of fear; I just lay back in complete surrender to the inevitable. Almost immediately I was surrounded by a brilliant light, brighter than sunshine, that filled my whole body with warmth, power and energy. As the light embraced me I asked in my mind, "Are you Gabriel?" But there was no reply.

I don't know how long the light was with me, but when I sat up and swung my legs over the bed, my mind was in turmoil – part of me wondering at the beauty and delight of the experience, part of me trying to decide what exactly had happened. Although the voices had told me it was God I was about to meet, somehow I had the impression that this was an angel. At the time I wondered whether this visitation meant that I was supposed to take up a spiritual vocation – an idea that made me very nervous indeed. I was a single mother with two children, trying hard to support my family as a dress designer: I couldn't see myself preaching to people about the Kingdom of God. Anyway, even if I had encountered a messenger from God, it was far from clear what the message was.

The experience stayed with me. I spent the next few weeks in a state of bliss and received many inner messages from the sweet voices – one of which was that I would meet someone I would marry. This state of consciousness was very beautiful and opened my eyes to the magic and glory of creation. I experienced the underlying unity of all apparently separate things and understood how everything that happens fits into a perfect pattern. But in this state it was impossible to live an ordinary life, and eventually I asked to be "brought back to earth". I had a sense of sadness about this, but shortly afterwards I met Will, the man to whom I have now been married for thirty-five years, and a new joy came into my life.

A few years later I went to live near Glastonbury, where I had another powerful experience. One summer afternoon in 1982, I was walking my baby in her pushchair down a country lane, when I felt the presence of a majestic being hanging in the air between heaven and earth, its feet on the rolling landscape, its head in the heavens. I didn't "see" this being, but when I was meditating next day I was surprised by an inner vision, which appeared suddenly in my mind, like a picture on a cinema screen. The image was of an angel walking in the English countryside. The angel's head, surrounded by a vast halo of radiant light, reached far into the heavens.

As I gazed at him I noticed some interesting details. The angel was wearing a white gown that shone as though made of some unearthly material. In one hand he carried an olive branch; in the other a large blue crystal. On his feet he wore plain brown sandals and in the landscape behind him, on the top of a hill, was a shining building that looked like some kind of temple. Behind him skipped a lamb, tiny beside his vast height.

In the 1980s there were no mind–body–spirit shelves in the bookshops, with a ready supply of books on angels, so I didn't go looking for information about this angel and I didn't talk to anyone about it – except my husband Will. To me, this was just a beautiful angel who had paid me a personal visit because I was meditating, and I didn't expect anyone else to be interested. But a few months later I came across an art book in the library – Angels *by Peter Lamborn Wilson – and as I flicked through I noticed one of the archangels was called Sandalphon. I had never come across this name before and I realized that the angel I had seen in my vision was Sandalphon.*

Over quite a few months I was privileged to have intimate meetings with other powerful spiritual beings and I felt I was being led on a very special journey. But I still thought it was a gift for me, personally. It never occurred to me that other people might be inspired by my process. But when you open the door to the angels, they will find plenty for you to do, so I very quickly found myself with a new gift to bring into the world via my books, channelled cards and now a new form of healing called Shefa healing. And it all started when I made a commitment to meditating every day!

William's story

William Bloom has become known as one of the UK's most experienced teachers, healers and authors in the field of holistic development. His work has helped thousands of people. He is the founder of the Foundation for Holistic Spirituality and I got to know him when I became interested in getting involved in his Spiritual Companions project, as well as through my work for spirituality in education.

When I was twenty-six years old I took two years' spiritual retreat in the High Atlas Mountains of southern Morocco, during which I focused on my relationship with the community of nature spirits, archetypes and angels. Later, after I had returned home to the UK, I was invited to lead some workshops at the Findhorn Foundation in Scotland, an innovative educational spiritual centre, which has a general acceptance of nature spirits and their importance for ecology, gardening and horticulture. I taught my first angels course there in the summer of 1983.

This first workshop consisted of fourteen women and ten men between the ages of eighteen and seventy-six. As they introduced themselves I was surprised by their maturity and intelligence. They were all working people and they had all had experiences that they wanted to clarify. They all had a distinct sense of cooperation and inspiration coming from an invisible dimension. They could feel that there was invisible support, but they wanted to understand it more clearly and also, if possible, to work more cooperatively with it.

What became clear was that there is a pattern of cooperation between humans and angels regardless of a person's background, culture or area of interest. Regardless of whether you are working as a healer, gardener, artist or business person, the way to cooperate with angels is always similar. It involves what we can call "attunement" and "invitation".

Attunement consists of taking a pause before any activity to tune into both the activity and its angel. Stop for a few minutes, become calm and quietly contemplate the activity you are about to undertake. At the same time relax and open yourself to sensing the essence or spirit of the activity. Many people do this instinctively. What may be new for you is to do this consciously.

So, for example, if you are going to garden, you take a few seconds' quiet time to contemplate both your garden and the spirits of gardening and of your garden. It would be exactly the same before doing a piece of art, or healing, or any other work. Then comes the "invitation" in which, during your moments of contemplation and attunement, you communicate an invitation to the spirits. In whatever way works for you, silently or spoken, call in the spirits. For example, "I call in the spirits of this garden." Or, "I call in the Angels of Healing." Then thank the spirit for being present with you as if it were already there. "Welcome and thank you for being with me."

Then, after this process of attunement and invitation, you just catch a sense of what you might do next. This is not a mental process, but is instinctive and intuitive. You have to get on with your gardening, or writing, or whatever it is – but in the quiet time of attunement you are open to impression. There is a rapport between your psyche and the energy field of the angel, and out of that comes an intuitive sense of what might be the best next action. Prune here. Paint with this colour. Ring this client first. And so on. You are not told what to do. You are magnetically attracted to act.

Recently, for example, I was writing my latest book and I kept getting stuck and frustrated with my lack of progress. Then – dah! – I remembered what I tell other people to do. I attuned to the book and its purpose, and I called in the angel of writing and good communications, Mercury. I thanked the spirit for its presence.

Just doing that completely changed the atmosphere and my attitude and, thankfully, I was able to write again and the text flowed. This angelic help for a writer is not surprising because another word for angel is "muse". Muses are precisely those spirits who help to inspire writers and artists, so there I was calling in my muse, and I am very happy and grateful to say that it did indeed help me.

Ishvara's story

Author, artist and angel workshop facilitator Ishvara D'Angelo had an angelic experience that subsequently changed her career from being a leading authority in aromatherapy to inspired "angel" artist. In May 1990 she was travelling home from an aromatherapy conference in America. She had also been attending teachings from His Holiness the Dalai Lama. Although the activities are totally separate, in light of what followed they have great significance.

Several hours into the flight, as the plane crossed the Atlantic in the middle of the night, Ishvara had an experience that changed her life. She saw an angel in the sky, in glorious glowing gold light. At first he seemed to be about the height of a tall man, but as she stared through the window he began expanding until he filled the whole sky. What she saw through her "visionary eyes" could not possibly have been seen from her position, for the golden being was sending beams of love to our planet, which to Ishvara's eyes had become small enough to see as a gently spinning globe.

First sketch

Although sceptics might suggest she was dreaming, it was the most powerful "dream" she had ever had, and as she looked at the angel through the window she made a thumbnail sketch of him. As she watched and absorbed the powerful experience she heard the words, "Go home and paint this."

Her life-changing experience was all the more significant because at that time she was a fully practising Buddhist and did not believe in God or angels. Having just spent time with His Holiness the Dalai Lama, angels could not have been further from her mind. Neither was it true that angels had appeared to her in a time of danger – the flight was smooth and (apart from this extraordinary experience) uneventful.

Ishvara went home and took out her brushes, which had not seen action in many years, and painted the picture. Very soon she had another vision of a vast feminine angel holding the earth, which she called "Universal Love". Once she had acknowledged the existence of angels, they ceased to appear externally as blazing lights but presented themselves as powerful mental images when she sat in meditation. And so Ishvara's life changed, from aromatherapy teacher and author to inspired artist. Her new identity even included a change of name.

The importance of names

Names are indeed important as they carry the vibrational energy of our very soul. It is not unusual for someone to change their name once they have had a spiritual awakening. More commonly, we begin to associate certain angels with particular names. The most popular names associated with angels are, of course, Michael and Gabriel, which are known in religious teachings by the Christian, Jewish and Muslim communities and are familiar throughout the world.

Aidan's story

Aidan Storey is a dedicated angel therapist, healer and clairvoyant whose work is highly regarded in his beautiful and spiritual homeland of Ireland, where we first met and became friends. His close connection with the angelic realms has been well documented in his own angel book. I enjoyed hearing his story of how his guardian angels interacted with him, telepathically communicating their names to him. By co-creating a distinct energy, which expressed their essence through feelings rather than words, Aidan was able to sense each of them, and give them an accurate human name.

My first long conversations with my guardian angels contained many questions, but this is one of my most memorable. It was a warm, still day and as I sat in my mother's garden the world seemed to become very quiet around me. As always, a beautiful white mist formed in front of me and within seconds two beautiful angels appeared and we began to speak in my mind. They explained to me that we always have at least two guardian angels around us.

"One guardian angel has been with you in every lifetime and a new one comes to you every time your soul is reborn, to help and guide you. I am the one who has walked with you in every lifetime." I asked the angel what I should call him and he explained that they don't have names in our human sense. But I was longing to hear some lengthy biblical names. "We don't have names. We don't possess any worldly titles. It is you humans who lovingly give us names. This makes you comfortable and it makes it easier for you to call on us. We love the earthy energy and the meaning these names carry," he said with a big smile.

"Right, I'll call you Zechariah. I feel that's a strong name and it suits you because you were always very strong when you came to me in my early days. You also made me strong and helped me cope better," I told the angel.

"I shall accept this beautiful name. Do you know its meaning?" he asked. I told the angel I didn't know the meaning of many names and felt a little foolish.

"It means 'God has remembered'. Isn't that glorious?" he said, very happy. I immediately realized (with a spine-tingling shiver) that I was intuitively picking up the vibration of the angel's name because deep down I knew that God had remembered me and sent the angel to help me.

My other angel's energy felt gentle and feminine – "I will call you Hannah. Is that OK?" I asked.

"Yes, I am very pleased. This name means 'graceful'. Thank you," she said.

"That is also beautiful. I picked these because they are among my favourite names and I felt they would suit you both and they do," I said. "Yes, beloved soul, they are very beautiful," Zechariah replied.

Averil's story

Another angel worker, who is very familiar with her angels and their names, is Averil James of Abergavenny. She works as a clairvoyant and healer with angel cards from her sanctuary at the bottom of her garden. I first met Averil and her husband when we all appeared together on TV.

I suppose it started about 1998 with workshops and sitting in a healing "circle" at Little Mill Spiritualist Group. We all went as a group to see Diana Cooper and I was impressed. I met a Reiki teacher and developed my healing potential, creating my own healing room with beautiful pictures of angels and crystals. Then I bought a book called Ask Your Angels. *To be honest, I didn't understand all of it, but the part I was most drawn to was about "automatic writing". So, I tried it for myself.*

My healer friends had encouraged me to protect my healing room with angels and to light a candle to bring in the angelic light. (It is said that with every candle you light, an angel appears.) I went into the room, lit a candle, asked my angels to come forward, sat at my desk, held a pencil to the paper and started.

From the very first moment the automatic writing just seemed to flow. I soon began to detect the same energies and, after a few moments of tuning in, they always started with the same sentence, which was "The path is clear and bright". I asked, "Who are you?" and was given three names: Solomon, a very strong and wise masculine energy; Michael, which felt different but again strong, protective and masculine; and then a very light and feminine angel called Amala.

I would ask a question and the replies were always really poetic. They would refer to "touching my heart" and always felt very loving. If I was worried or troubled I would ask a question. For example, when I left my job and decided to become a self-employed angel-card reader and clairvoyant, I was concerned whether I would be able to make a living. The answer came, "The people will come from far and wide" and, in fact, that is now very true.

One evening I was sitting watching a film when I felt I needed to switch off as the automatic writing was coming through. I took up a pen and the writing became very fast and frantic, but I was feeling "pictures" rather than words. It was very different handwriting to my own and I had the message, "Ella is with us surrounded by light and entertaining everyone". I knew that was a message about my mother, who had recently died. I knew in my heart that these were messages from angels and not spirit guides. They always gave me beautiful poetic words, expressing the creative energy of universal love. It has been wonderful. Although I felt they were just for me, very personal, I am happy to share this with you now – there may be other people who receive these automatic messages and who might be reassured by my experience.

From angels writing beautiful messages to another type of muse. About six years after that first sighting, our artist friend, Ishvara, experienced another angel "out there" – all the others had been inner visions.

I had just bought a house that needed a lot of work and I'd had to sack the builder who'd started on the job but failed to turn up most days. Then I received a call to tell me that a correspondence course on which I was a tutor was about to close, so I was suddenly going to be some £9,000 a year worse off. I was tearing my hair out. A few days later I turned from the lounge into the hallway and there was an angel, dancing, with what I can only describe as a cheeky grin on her face! I recognized her at once, as I had seen her painted on the ceiling of a chapel in Siena on my very first trip to Italy.

For the next few days I walked about with a big grin on my face, too! I might have been broke and in need of funds for the building work, but I'd got an angel who danced in my hall. Then everything began to get better: the surveyors refunded the fee I'd paid them and I discovered that one of my former students was married to a builder, who turned out to be efficient, honest and sensitive. Two of my sons came from hundreds of miles away and did the plumbing and tiling work, and I decided to knock out all the rotten plaster myself so that I would only have to pay for the replastering.

As I took a big hammer to the plaster, I realized that the traditional lathes were still behind– the ideal support for a fresco. I had taken two fresco-painting courses in Italy and was inspired to paint one of the dancing angel in the hallway, where I had seen her. So I asked my nice builder to leave a panel empty and I painted my dancing angel at the foot of the stairs, where she had first appeared.

Not long after I'd finished the fresco, a very wise clairvoyant friend came to supper and he channelled the information that this angel was not only guarding my house, but the whole hillside on which it was built. Years later I sold the house and the new owner, who knew nothing of that conversation, sent me a Christmas card the following year, saying "Your angel still guards the house!"

But that isn't the end of the story. A firm of developers submitted plans for a huge new housing development, which would have radically changed the area where the house stood. The residents put up a spirited fight and, in the end, they won. Just after that I met a former neighbour, who'd been at the forefront of the planning appeal and was jubilant – not surprisingly. But what was surprising was that she said, "Ishvara, I think your angel had a lot to do with it." Now, she was a person who had never, as far as I knew, showed any interest in angels or, indeed, anything of a spiritual nature. I told her how my friend had said, all those years before, that the angel was there for the whole hillside – the hillside that would have been covered with houses if the planning application had succeeded – and she smiled and nodded.

Sarah's story

Sometimes angels appear with far more cryptic gifts, such as in the case of my close friend, Maggie, whose daughter, Sarah, had a visitation when she was about seven years old. She came down for breakfast one morning telling her mummy that she had been woken up in the middle of the night by music. Maggie tells the story.

Sarah said that music had woken her from her sleep and when I asked her what kind of music she told me that it was the angels singing. I was already aware that Sarah had some psychic ability from things she had said as a tiny girl. I asked her what they looked like. "Very white and bright, like lights," she told me. She had tried to see their faces because she thought they would be pretty, but the light was too bright. "Did they say anything to you, Sarah?" I asked her. "They spoke in a language that I didn't understand, but I knew what they were saying to me – they told me that I am here to do something special, Mummy, and that I will remember when the time is right."

Although at twenty-one Sarah has many musical achievements, she hasn't stumbled across her "right time" – yet.

When my goddaughter, Caitlin, was expected, her mother, Iren, could hear music in certain areas of the house throughout the whole pregnancy. Being highly sensitive and very spiritual herself she immediately understood it to be the angels of her unborn child assisting the transition of her soul into this lifetime. When Caitlin arrived, following an extremely difficult birth, the angels continued to sing, and Iren heard music above the baby's cot for several months. At six years old

Caitlin often "sees" fairies and lights, with which she seems to be very comfortable.

My mother's story

Psychic connections and children seem to be a theme in my family. One of the big questions of life relates to "destiny". Some of us seem to have a role to play by creating dramatic effects in our lives, while others can spread calm and love around them just by being there. Is our life mapped out for us by God, or even decided by our own soul, before we arrive on earth? Do we create our destiny as it evolves, for ourselves and sometimes for our children by the choices we make at each crossroads? Who knows the road ahead? I am sure that the angels do! My grandma used to tell me of how she bargained for my mother's life and got her back from the dead. Sounds like a tall story? You decide for yourself.

My mother, Sylvia, was born in 1929 and was an only child. She was a sensitive little girl, who was often poorly. Like many young northern families, my grandparents were hit hard during the 1930s depression and had to make do with inferior food and little heating. My mother caught brucellosis. Unable to afford a doctor, my grandma nursed her alone, but my mother's condition rapidly worsened and the situation became so severe that my grandfather was sent to negotiate with the doctor, who came after his rounds.

My mother had lost consciousness. By the time the doctor arrived it was too late and my grandma knew she was losing her only child. She began to pray arduously and as she pleaded for the life of her daughter she made a promise to God. She begged God to allow her to keep this child as she had already lost her second baby a few months before. In return, my grandma offered her daughter in service and promised that whatever talent she displayed as a gift she would make sure it was used in His name.

What happened next is quite remarkable. The doctor pronounced my mother dead. But my grandma could see her standing next to her body talking with a bright light. As her little girl began to fade away toward the light, she turned and suddenly came back into her body. Sylvia took a breath and woke up.

Reunited

My mother says she can recall the memory with extreme clarity. She had felt so light and joyful and she found herself in a beautiful garden full of trees. There were people in the distance and although she knew she ought to recognize them she couldn't make out who they were, as if they were vaguely transparent. She crossed a bridge, where she recognized a male figure walking toward her and she was overjoyed at reuniting with someone whom she now refers to as her spiritual father. She stood for a while and spoke with him as he explained she must return to the family she had chosen, as there was much work for her to complete during her lifetime. Reluctantly, she came back.

As she grew up Sylvia became a highly talented musician, playing the concert piano and training to become an operatic soprano at the Royal Academy of Music. Later she won many competitions and eventually appeared at the new National Theatre in London at the opening ceremony of the Festival of Britain in 1953. However, though music may have been a gift from the angels, it was not the service she had been required to fulfil and later she developed the spiritual healing and channelling skills that became her life's work. Did my grandmother's prayers and faith have an effect on Sylvia's destiny, or was her path already created?

Mark's story

The angelic muse of music led another friend, Mark, to discover a world of angels, which added a whole new dimension to his life and work when he entered a music competition and won.

In June 2001 Mark Hughes, a business entrepreneur and part-time singer-songwriter, was asked to write a song for a new event to be staged in London called World Angel Day. The event would be the first of its kind, held to celebrate the existence of angels. Speakers, authors and musicians from around the world would be appearing at this first World Angel Day.

The planned event would become reality just four months later, in October 2001, and the organizers wanted a song that would capture the essence of the celebration of angels. They decided to hold a competition to choose the best song for World Angel Day.

Mark composed "The Angel Song" late one night that June, put together a studio demo and sent it off to the organizers. Being a family man, with an incredibly busy life, he forgot about the song and the event and, not having heard anything by October, assumed that his song had not been chosen. Then one day in early October he received a call from Diana Cooper, who was the main inspiration behind World Angel Day, telling him that from over a hundred entries Mark's song had been chosen. She also asked him if he would perform it at World Angel Day – only six days away.

This would have been a tall order even if Mark had been rehearsing the song already, but he hadn't played or sung it since the recording session in June. However, he agreed to perform it and went about preparing in the short time left.

White feathers

Early on the Friday morning before the event Mark came out of his house to go to work and was faced with an incredible sight. The canvas roof of his convertible car was covered in about a hundred pure-white feathers. Describing the sight Mark said, "It was as if two white doves had fought on top of the car and then flown off, leaving just their feathers. Amazingly, there were none on the ground, the boot or the bonnet." Mark was baffled and, at that time, not aware of the significance of white feathers in relation to angels. He called his wife, Amanda, out to see the feathers and she was as surprised as he was, but thinking no more about it, he drove off to work.

Two days later, on the Sunday of World Angel Day, Mark and Amanda arrived at Kensington Town Hall and took their seats in the area reserved for performers and participants. Diana Cooper opened the event and the very first thing she spoke about was the significance of white feathers. She explained that they are considered the angels' calling cards and a sign that angels are there, helping us. It's not difficult to imaging the look on Mark and Amanda's faces. As he said, "If one white feather means that angels are there helping us, then I certainly had plenty of help that day!"

Significantly, the lyrics of Mark's composition, "The Angel Song", go like this: "There are angels watching over me and you, guiding us home, seeing us through. Anytime, any day, anywhere, anyway, there are angels, there are angels, there are angels watching over you."

How true.

For the greater good

I know, through my own experiences, how much the angels assist us in our everyday organization, in particular when we are doing something "for the greater good", such as charity work. When we agree to take part in a selfless act, for a higher purpose, the angels gather and as we call they come closer to enable us to really make a difference. One of my students wrote to tell me how she connected with the angels and just how much they helped her on a recent charity trip from Land's End to John o'Groats.

The planning for this sponsored cycle ride from Land's End to John o'Groats started last summer, after three of my nephews decided to do something to raise funds for a charity, Cancer Research UK. I immediately offered to go along as support – as a trained therapist I knew that aromatherapy massage and Reiki would be needed along the way.

In January, just before I started working with angels, I sent out an email to all my friends in the Reiki world, asking them to put this trip on their Reiki grids with the intention of a safe, happy, healthy trip and the most appropriate weather conditions for the ride. I then bought a big map of the UK, plotted out the route from Land's End to John o'Groats and wrote my intention on the map.

Then in March I met Chrissie and the whole world of angels opened up before me. I started using the Angel Insight *cards every day, for meditation, picking a card for the day and doing readings. Once I had a little practice I did a reading for the cycle ride, wrote down all that came to me during the reading and also put that on my Reiki grid. At the end of April we set off for Land's End. On a very misty evening we dropped the cyclists off at Land's End to cycle the first 3 miles to the campsite before starting their ride in earnest the next day.*

The next morning the weather was lovely and sunny and off they set on this epic ride. For the next fourteen days this was the routine: the cyclists set off and I would pack up and start driving to the next campsite. Each morning during the drive I would talk to the angels. First I would thank them for the day before, thank them for the weather and thank them for the fact that we were all safe and healthy, with a positive attitude and good team spirit.

Then I would ask Archangel Michael to put a bubble of light around the cyclists and keep them safe, and ask the same for myself in my campervan and my sister and her husband in their motor home. Then I would ask Archangel Michael to keep everyone else on the road safe. I would ask the angels to keep the cyclists dry and motivated and maintain the good team spirit. I would also ask the angels to keep everyone at home safe and free from worry.

At the end of the day, when we met the cyclists, they were always very upbeat. Even though the cycling was tough, they had stayed dry all day and always found some funny stories to tell about what had happened along the way. As we settled into a routine, they would say to me, "I don't know what you are doing, but just keep doing it because it is working."

Riding through Scotland they could see cloud and rain all around, but not where they were. Once it did start to hail and there, next to them, was a large oak tree, big enough for three cyclists and their bikes. There was not another large tree for miles.

One day I had gone to pick up the cyclists as the campsite was off the route. They had got separated in a busy town and I wasn't sure where they all were, so I sent out a plea to Archangel Michael, asking him to guide me to them. Sitting at this busy roundabout I decided to take the next exit and 100 yards up the road was one of the cyclists. I managed to pull into a small car park, which just happened to be there, and after ten minutes the others appeared.

At the end of the trip, we had driven or cycled nearly 1,000 miles, the cyclists had only had three punctures, one each, one cyclist had fallen off twice, both at a standstill when he couldn't get his foot out of his pedal – once onto a flower bed and once onto a grass verge. There were no injuries, no accidents and they had stayed dry. We had all bonded as a team, looking after each other along the way.

It just goes to show what a difference it makes asking for help from angels, setting the intention, remaining focused and thanking the angels every day. Mind you, on the last day I thought they'd finish at about five o'clock, so asked for dry weather until then. They arrived later, at 5.30pm, and the heavens opened – but a rainbow appeared. Now that, I thought, was very cool!

And so welcome to the mystery of co-creation! As the talents and abilities that we often hadn't even recognized gradually unfold, those light-bulb moments create even more joy in our hearts and minds as we begin to realize our potential.

I hope that these stories have served to inspire you and reaffirm your own magical ability to take your part in the ever-changing creation of your universe. We can do anything – all we need is an open heart, and to trust.

Meditation for Creativity

This meditation is to connect you the energies of the beautiful Archangel Jophiel.

- Begin by sitting comfortably, with your feet on the ground. Breathe in and out so that the in-breath and the out-breath are the same length. Breathing in your favourite colour. Breathing out any tension, worries, anxieties – let them all go.
- Breathing in and breathing out – with each out-breath allow your neck and shoulders to relax. Allow your arms to rest comfortably on your thighs with your palms facing upward, and relax. As you breathe in your favourite colour, imagine it passing down through your body, down your arms and your legs. Do this until the colour comes out through your skin and you can imagine yourself sitting as a bright being of beautiful colour. In your imagination, turn

this to a bright sunny yellow, so your whole being is surrounded by sunshine-yellow light. Imagine that you can see the light. Feel it around your face, on your skin, as the light becomes brighter and brighter. Visualize the sun and imagine how strong it is. As you embrace the light, think about how bright, how beautiful, how warm, how life-giving is sunlight.

- Think about how strong the light from the sun is in our eyes – if you can't stare directly at the sun, imagine how much stronger the light from God must be!
- Imagine yourself walking through a beautiful garden and finding a place to sit down. As you sit – noticing the flowers, feeling the sunshine on your skin, smelling a fragrance, watching butterflies flutter around – enjoy the freedom of being on your own in this special, sacred place. Immerse yourself in the wonder of creation.
- Imagine that you turn, and as you do so you see a being walking toward you, a being so bright, so tall – this must be an angel. Try to see the angel's face – but the light is so bright. The being walks toward you. How do you feel in this light? The angel tells you that he or she represents the angels of the realm belonging to creativity, governed by Archangel Jophiel.
- Ask the angel to inspire you, to illuminate your mind. Ask for a message that will help you develop your creative powers, to give you a sense of your own creativity.
- Ask the angel to give you a message in the form of a symbol or a sign to inspire you so that you can, in your way, be part of creation.

- As pictures or colours or words or sensations come into your mind or your skin, thank the angel. Bathe in this beautiful golden light and with a sense of gratitude, as the angel walks away, allow yourself to remember all the beautiful things that you have seen, that you have been part of. Think of how creativity comes into your life. Do you like art? Do you like writing or poetry? Do you love making your home beautiful? Are you involved in a creative process that is helping to preserve this beautiful planet of ours? Take yourself to your favourite place, full of happy memories, colours, fragrances and sounds and stay with that moment. Allow yourself to feel the joy of that memory. Breathe it down into your body as an inner smile and a lasting joy.
- Now take yourself back to the garden, where you're sitting among all the flowers, trees, butterflies, birds. Give yourself a moment of inner peace and tranquillity. Breathing deeply, bring your consciousness back into this place where you are now sitting. Feeling your feet on the ground, bring the energy back into your body as you breath deeply.
- And when you're ready, very gently, open your eyes.

"Angel of Air, breathe through me and inspire me with the beauty of all creation."

CHAPTER 6

GIFTS OF COURAGE

Courage is a very subjective quality. Do you remember how, in the film *The Wizard of Oz*, the dear gentle lion felt he wasn't brave enough and set out to find "courage"? When we need more courage to overcome fear from whomever or whatever frightens us, we must remember that there is only love. If we are in a place of love then fear has no hold on us. Archangel Zadkiel and his angels will help you to change all negative thoughts into positive action. By being positive we automatically feel more courageous. Asking the angels to give us courage also creates more confidence, and in turn enables us to turn from fear and put love into action.

"The angels know we are user-friendly, they simply follow the instructions written in our heart."

Each of us has incredible personal power. We are capable of creating and manifesting our dreams. We can change lives; we can build and destroy, grow and heal, reproduce our race and change history. We have immense power and can reach great and wonderful heights of achievement. Yet many of us do not recognize our power and feel we lack the courage needed to reach our personal goals. The angels can help give us courage. They support and empower us and give us strength whenever we feel weak. All we have to do is believe, just as children do.

While many people have had life-changing experiences that they attribute to the angels because they relate the events to religious teachings or the spiritual world, children, in their wonderful innocence, often describe angelic visitations without any prior knowledge. The angels make their presence known to children often as another child or as a caring female presence.

Whether the visitation is to give protection, guidance or courage, we usually refer to these angels as our "guardian" angels. The next two stories illustrate how children are closely connected with their guardian angels, and how angels appear to gently give them courage and reassurance – with or without their parents' knowledge.

Sue's story

One day, a heavily pregnant woman came to find me at a mind, body and spirit event in the Midlands. I had a stand selling angel books and ceramic figures and I also gave a talk about guardian angels during the day. The young woman, whom we can call Sue, was clearly upset and wanted to talk to someone about the presence of angels. She had come to the show specifically to find someone to help her. A self-confessed agnostic, with no particular belief or faith, she had no knowledge of anything spiritual and was very confused.

Sue explained that her marriage had been troubled and that her husband had recently left, after she gave up work to have their second baby. Her first child, Ben, aged four, had been very sad since his daddy had gone away. He had not eaten well, couldn't sleep and even refused to play with his toys or watch his favourite TV programmes. Sue was beside herself with worry, not just financially, but also for the welfare of her new baby and her son.

She had remembered reading a magazine article about the help of angels and when she saw a poster advertising the event and my talk, she came to find out more. She would never normally have come to an event like this. Purely by "coincidence" she had seen the advertisement for my talk and felt drawn to speak to me.

During the week prior to the fair, Ben had come down from his room one evening, after he had been put to bed, and said, "Mummy there is a shiny lady in my room, all dressed in white, who knows who I am, she calls me Ben. I don't know what she wants, but she keeps smiling and talking to me."

Frantically, and with only fear in her mind, Sue had rushed upstairs and into Ben's bedroom, but of course she found no one there. She didn't know what to do about the "imaginary" visitor. Half believing that it was a ghost she became frightened herself. It hadn't occurred to her that it might have been an angel.

This same occurrence had happened night after night throughout the week. Yet Ben seemed to be regaining his former cheerful self. He stopped mentioning the "shining lady" for a couple of days, until one morning he came down to say to worried Sue, "It's all right, Mummy. The shiny lady says we have to be brave and everything will be OK now. And it will, Mummy, because she is SO beautiful."

Following the visit of the "beautiful white lady", Ben rediscovered his normal happy self, playing, eating and sleeping like a healthy little boy again. Could it be that this is what is meant by the teaching that we need to return to the trusting innocence of a child in order to actually see the angels for ourselves, and gain from their presence?

Daniel's story

You may have heard of the Christian saying, "Dare to be a Daniel!" My son, Dan, certainly fits into that category. As he was walking by the age of ten months and climbing out of his cot by a year old, it was always easy to see how adventurous and capable he would become, and how many scrapes he might get into later.

Daniel spent his childhood and teens wanting to be a stunt man. Indeed, the headmistress of his nursery school told me one day to brace myself for the future, as from her experience of little boys, she feared (this was said with a grin!) that this one would either join a circus or the SAS.

He climbed and jumped from anything that was taller than him. He hid objects, sometimes alive and willing, such as the tortoise, his little sister and himself, in any sizeable container that would roll along or fit onto his plastic bulldozer. He could ride a two-wheeled bike by the age of four and a half. Daniel's adventures were hilarious to watch, but clearly promised future challenges. Luckily, his two fairly adventurous Aries parents were rarely fazed by his antics.

One year, celebrating the Chinese New Year in London and watching the fighting dragons, Daniel was delighted to learn that he was born in the Year of the Monkey. He decided that this was why he was so good at climbing trees – any playtime in the park was punctuated by my instructions of, "Daniel, concentrate and hold tight", or "Daniel, for goodness' sake get down!"

Little Dan's life was saved on more than one occasion. The story I am about to share was one of the most miraculous and one that made me truly believe and trust in the power of the angels to hold life in the palm of their hand, giving us both the gift of knowing that courage should be used wisely.

A lucky escape

One day Daniel decided to climb the lofty old pear tree at the bottom of our garden. He was five years old. I was in the kitchen washing up and had watched him racing toward the tree on his little bike. Within seconds he was climbing into the lower branches and heading swiftly further up. My heart sank as I felt a shudder of anticipation of impending disaster – in my mind's eye I had a fleeting vision of him falling. As I ran out of the kitchen and down to the bottom of our 80ft garden to call out to Daniel to stop, the small branches at the top of the tree where he was climbing had already snapped.

He lost his hold and fell with a thud onto his back. For a few seconds he lay motionless as I rushed toward him. Then he stood up and, although breathless, gave me a worried grin. "I'm OK, Mummy." I saw where he had fallen and my brain started to process the incredible and miraculous accuracy of his landing in such a tiny space.

Immediately behind and below the branches of this big old tree was our glass greenhouse. Right in front of the tree was a raised rockery garden with large sharp, jagged stones. To the side was a small flight of concrete steps. Daniel had fallen directly into the soft patch of grass inside the triangle of protruding roots at the base of the tree. This area of grass measured no more than 1ft across.

Unbelievably he was unscathed, if a little shaken. My instant reaction was to pick him up and thank God and the angels with all my heart. If I had seen a hand gently guide him down to that tiny patch of soft ground I would not have been surprised. Daniel's mantra became, "I'm a really lucky boy, aren't I, Mummy!"

The lion's den

In this next escapade of a little boy facing adversity, the vision of angels was mine, but the courageous tale of angelic protection and courage was of Daniel in this modern version of a lion's den.

When Dan was diagnosed with diabetes at seven years old, his dad and I were determined that he should live as normal a life as possible. We wanted him to enjoy doing all the things every other healthy little boy would do. This included school trips, sports, beaver-scouts, birthday parties and anything else that came along.

My husband had been very much in denial about the diabetes and refused to accept that there was anything seriously wrong with his son, even though type-1 diabetes is a life-threatening condition. As a mother I felt a huge amount of guilt that, as a trained nurse, I had not picked up on the signs myself.

Daniel had been losing weight, but I put that down to a growth spurt. He had also become miserable when he was thirsty for quite some time, and had complained of blurred vision (which the optician dismissed as a common form of attention-seeking), but it wasn't until his teacher called me to school to let me know that Daniel needed to visit the loo far too often that I took him for tests and found him to be insulin-dependent. From that time on he carried an ample supply of fruit drinks and glucose bars and was well rehearsed in letting anyone know about his diabetes in games and out-of-school activities.

I took Daniel to alternative practitioners, too, and they all helped a great deal. He was successfully coping; even as a seven-year-old he insisted on doing his own injections and became a mini-authority on the benefits of acupuncture, Chinese herbal teas, cranial osteopathy and visualization techniques. Even if Daniel didn't understand the technicalities, he certainly knew how much the different practices were helping him.

An exciting day trip

That first summer he and his sister, Claire, were booked into holiday club activities for the first two weeks of the summer break. They went along with friends and I was happy with the arrangements. The really exciting trip came at the end of the first week: it was a day trip to Woburn Safari Park.

The park is huge, with many square miles of water, open grazing, the wildlife safari and a stately home. There is a funfair, a boating lake and many other attractions to thrill a family and I was sorry I couldn't go along, too. My friend and I delivered our children to the holiday club centre, along with packed lunches and, for Daniel, his insulin injections, water and between-meal snacks. I went to work.

That evening I duly arrived to collect my children, to be met by a grave little Claire telling me that Daniel was missing. I just smiled. I was so used to his mischief I simply said, "Come on, stop teasing and tell me where he is. We have to go back to work and help Daddy with the parcels." But no, on this occasion he did not leap out shouting, "Boo!" He wasn't hiding. He wasn't waiting for his mummy.

I looked at the group leader, whose face was ashen. "Mrs Hulme, I don't know what to say. We don't seem to have Daniel with us and I don't know where he is," he told me, literally wringing his hands.

"When did you last see him?" I asked calmly.

"One of the children saw him get off the minibus to nip to the toilets, just before we left Woburn, but he didn't tell a member of staff and it was after the head count.

So it seems we drove off without him." Then, in the ensuing excitement, another child called out that she thought she had seen Daniel at the motorway services, on the toilet stop halfway back to London.

There had been two minibuses and several car loads driven by staff members, each one thinking the group complete. But he was a vivacious child, fun of fun and exuberant laughter. He could not be missed. They were also all aware of the seriousness of Daniel's newly diagnosed diabetes. Surely, I thought, someone must have taken responsibility for his care and realized he wasn't there?

I was as calm as a cucumber on the surface, but I could feel a volcano of hysteria welling up inside. It was imperative that we wasted no more time. We had discovered Daniel was missing, now something had to be done. I suggested that the staff telephone the safari park security and the transport police at the motorway services.

Pre-internet, it was slow finding the correct telephone numbers for any of these services. I didn't have a mobile phone, so I wasn't even able to contact my husband. However, I contacted a business associate, Carole, who was able to help get in touch with him. In the meantime I was fully aware that this was a Friday evening, the first weekend of the summer holidays and a beautiful July day, and that all roads northbound would be packed. There would be no chance of me reaching Woburn for several hours.

The transport police at the service station had found no trace of a small boy answering Dan's description. He was friendly, chatty, bonny, blond and blue-eyed. All the media hype about missing children flashed through my head and alarm bells rang loudly in my ears.

The security guys on the park gates had not seen him. The police had not seen him. Oh my poor little lost boy! In the park there were lions, lakes with boats to climb on and any number of dangers for a wandering, adventurous seven-year-old. I imagined him drowning at best, being mauled by a lion at worst. And I was all too familiar with diabetes and the dangers of him having no food, water or insulin with him. His bag had been found when it returned on the bus without him.

I arranged for one of the staff members to take my daughter home and to stay there to answer the phone and distract Claire until we had Daniel back safely. The poor little mite was very upset and felt she was to blame for her brother's disappearance. I jumped in my car to drive back to work to find my husband, who until this point was unaware of the situation.

My heart was pounding as I sped off back to east London, pleading to God that my son would be safe. Frankly, looking back now, I'm not sure how I was able to drive in a straight line as the tears were flooding down my cheeks, my heart was pounding through my chest and my stomach was churning with anxiety.

A sign

Then, as I slowed down to leave the motorway, there in front me, shining directly at me in the sky was a huge cross of bright white light. For a moment I stared in awe and amazement. Instantly recognizing the symbol of the cross, I became completely calm. I had never thought of the crucifix as a symbol of anything other than Christ's love, so although its appearance shocked me it did not alarm me. The cross turned into a white figure with outstretched arms. I wasn't sure whether it was an angel or a vision of Jesus. Beautiful, dressed in a bright white robe and smiling, his arms and hands reached out toward me as he called to me, gently shaking his head, "Christine, Christine, how could you think I would let anything happen to your son Daniel? Take courage, my dear one."

The vision faded. I have no idea how long it lasted. Split seconds, perhaps. I was driving, after all, and I certainly had not stopped. As the vision disappeared, so did my fear and I drove on to make the necessary plans to find our son, confident in the knowledge that he would be safe.

I was furious and disappointed in my husband, who wouldn't agree to setting off immediately to try to find him ourselves. He wouldn't leave his work until it was complete. On the other hand, we had listened to the bulletins on the radio and knew that the motorways were jammed with holiday traffic. I took control and remained in contact with the security guards, the police, the motorway police and my friend Carole over the next two hours.

Found safe and well

Eventually, three hours that seemed like an eternity later, at around 9pm, we had a call to say that Daniel had been found. One of the security cameras had picked up his image as he approached the main house at Woburn. He had knocked on the front door of the majestic stately home, a security guard had seen him on camera and he had informed the staff inside. As the door opened, he said, "Hello, I'm Daniel, and I'm diabetic. I need some food!" The landowner himself welcomed him in and his butler made him a sandwich and chatted to him in the grand kitchen until the security officers made contact with the police, Carole and eventually ourselves.

The little chap had seen his minibus drive off without him at around four o'clock. After a moment or two of worried tears he convinced himself that someone would come back for him, so he sat and waited. Then, he went back on the fairground rides. He had seen the sign saying "Last ride 6pm" and so, when all the rides finished, he knew it was six o'clock. As the gates closed, with families and groups heading toward the car parks, he felt very lost and didn't know what to do. Trusting and waiting he decided to walk round to one of the other gates to see if there was anyone there.

As he was telling me I realized that the poor child had never been taught how to make a reverse-charge call by public phone. Isn't it funny how you don't know what you don't know, until you find out you didn't know it? I also understood how my instructions not to talk to strangers had somewhat backfired. When I asked him why he hadn't gone to the park staff he pointed out that everyone he saw was a stranger. So he courageously just kept walking and walking, knowing that eventually his mummy would come and find him.

We finally rescued our little hero from our colleagues in Luton well after midnight. Daniel and I were both exhausted by the experience, and I just wanted to hold onto him and reassure him with thousands of cuddles. The possible dangers were many. Daniel had clearly been well guarded and encouraged by his angels that day.

My gratitude to the divine source of infinite love and care was indescribable – beyond words. My son told his adventure story for years. In accordance with the laws of karma, Daniel has since saved the life of a dear friend during a diving accident, and also of two other strangers. But these are stories for another time. I am happy that he still believes in the guardianship of angels at the age of thirty.

Debbie's story

Sometimes the gifts we receive are more tangible – we receive an actual material gift from the angels to give us encouragement and confidence. These gifts are always highly symbolic, as told here by one of my former students, who received a beautiful gift of encouragement that was left behind after a strange angelic visitation.

I collapsed on my bed, utterly exhausted, wondering how I'd get through the next day, let alone the next year. It was the late 1980s and I'd endured an acrimonious divorce, which had dragged through an eight-year court case. To make things worse, after splitting up with my husband and moving out with my two young children, my weight had plummeted to just 6 stone and I was weak and worn out. I pleaded with my guardian angels, spirits and guides, and anyone out there listening, to help me turn my life around.

As I lay on my bed with my eyes closed the night before the final court hearing, I suddenly heard a noise in the room. It sounded like the flutter of wings. I am terrified of birds and my first thought was that one must have flown down the chimney. The fluttering became louder and louder, until it sounded as if the bird was right above my face. Very nervously I opened my eyes.

To my astonishment, I saw a massive white wing gently fanning up and down. As my eyes adjusted to the bright light a winged man with a yellow glow around his head came into focus. He was hovering mid-air and wearing a white gown. He had short blond hair and sky-blue eyes. My fear left me as he beamed at me with the kindest smile. A feeling of peace and warmth washed over me. The constant knot of nerves I had been feeling in my stomach melted away and I instantly knew that everything was going to be all right in the end. I smiled back at the angel as he hovered for a few more moments and then disappeared backward through the wall.

The next morning, my daughter burst into my bedroom clutching something tightly in her hand. "Mummy, the man asked me to give you this," she said, before placing something in my hand. "You know the man in white who comes to visit? He said to tell you everything is going to be OK." I was surprised to see that she'd given me a pewter charm of a winged horse, which I later found out was Pegasus. I had never seen it before, but I slipped it onto a silver chain and immediately fastened it round my neck before I went to court that morning.

Thankfully, the case went in my favour, lifting a huge weight from my shoulders. I still wear the charm to this day, and feel so comforted when I hold it in my hand. I am so grateful the angel answered my call and appeared to me as a comfort during such a difficult time. I know that one day I will meet him again.

Pegasus, the winged horse, is one of the many symbols of good triumphing over evil: he is a beautiful white horse with angelic wings. We find the Pegasus image in art all through the ages and he is known for his courage and beauty. Many wanted to tame him, but he eluded all their efforts.

Louise's story

The next story may surprise you. Think of a symbol for winning the race, crawling at a snail's pace or carrying the world on your back and you may find yourself thinking of a snail or a tortoise. The tortoise is also, in esoteric terms, the symbol of wisdom. Able to defend itself on its own, it personifies water, the moon, Mother Earth, time, immortality and fertility.

In the chapter on gifts of protection (see pages 67–70), I told you about the story of Louise and the doorbell that rang three times at our house. On a later occasion her angels presented her with another very real symbol of their closeness and guardianship. It is also a clear example of how the angels never give up on us, even when we seem to repeat the same unfortunate patterns in our lives. They have ultimate patience and will continue to help us over and over again.

Louise and her two children had returned to her partner and although, at first, they worked hard to repair the damage done by previous arguments, she felt that her life was not on the right track. She felt disconnected from any spiritual life and, back in her partner's home, was feeling frustrated and controlled. She had been asking the angels for a sign of how to resolve her situation for the best outcome. She knew she needed to find a home of her own, where she felt totally safe.

The next day Louise went for a walk with her partner and their dog. Her partner went one way to jog around the fields and wood, while Louise decided that she would rather walk straight through the wood with the dog, as she loved the shade of the high beech trees in the early summer heat.

The tortoise

Strolling along the pathway toward the wood Louise called out to God and the angels, "Please help me, show me a sign that you are still here at least! I need to know what to do." Distracted by the behaviour of the dog, her thoughts suddenly changed and she found herself thinking back to when she had been very young, and how she had always wanted a tortoise as a pet. "Ha," she thought, "now a tortoise, why am I thinking about a tortoise? But that would be lovely, I would have so liked to have had a tortoise!" She thought about her disappointment at not being allowed to have one as a child.

As Louise walked into the woods her dog began sniffing at a lump in the grass. "Come on boy," she called, "leave!" The dog was not going to leave; this find was far too interesting. When she went over to investigate, Louise could not believe her eyes. There in the grass was a tortoise. Away from the village and beyond, nestling in the undergrowth, as large as life, was a lovely old tortoise.

Louise knew straight away that this was the sign she had been pleading for, and picked up the tortoise to take home for her son to look after. In its bizarre nature, this was clearly a significant sign for her, and one not easily ignored. She had a feeling that something was going to happen and probably soon. She knew that the angels had materialized this tortoise to show her that they were capable of anything and were encouraging her to believe that everything would work out. The angels had heard her. They would help her through and she must have courage to be strong, just like this little lost tortoise with its home on its back.

Sure enough, as if by design, the very next day her partner lost his temper once again and ordered Louise and her two children out of "his" house. In desperation Louise called me from outside her barred door and we welcomed her and her children into our home. Within three days they had found somewhere else to live and moved into a rented cottage, with the help of friends – angelic and earthly.

Alison's story

Sometimes courage comes in the form of divine inspiration and sometimes it is the confidence to know how to do something, as in Alison's story of her flat tyre.

I was at an all-time low and most things seemed to be going wrong in my life. I had been ill and arguing with my partner and my work situation was depressing me. Generally things were deteriorating badly.

It was a Saturday morning and my car MOT was due. My partner always took the car in for me, but because things were so bad between us, I felt on this occasion I had to go with him. He had spent the previous day preparing the car and it was all ready, but when we went to the car, we couldn't believe it – there was a flat tyre. So my partner got the spare out and changed the tyre, while I stood and daydreamed. I had never changed a tyre in my life and really had no idea what he was doing – I had absolutely no interest either. He changed the tyre and the car passed its MOT.

Six days later, I was driving to the south of Ireland, alone. I left very early in the morning and was driving down a motorway when something felt wrong. I pulled off down a country road, possibly the silliest thing to have done in the circumstances. I had another flat tyre and there was no one around. I was in the middle of nowhere, a long way from home and alone.

I just didn't know what to do and panicked. Yes, there were tears! I tried to remember how the tyre had been changed the previous week, but couldn't. I got the spare and the parts out and stared at them, wondering what on earth I was supposed to do with them.

My heart sank. I was panicking and really the only thing I could do was ask my angels for help. I was annoyed and probably not the most pleasant person for them to deal with. I think I even blamed them for letting me get into that situation. I was angry and scared and, yet, even in the middle of that, I felt a change in the energy around me. I became calm and when I looked down, a little white feather floated past my feet, right in front of the flat tyre.

I was ecstatic and scooped it up in my hand. It's difficult to explain, but it was as if I was on automatic pilot. I began to change the tyre. I felt as if it wasn't me doing this – I didn't know how to. The repair happened in stages. The first stage was raising the car, but I found it too difficult. I seemed to know what to do, but didn't have the strength. I just kept asking for help and I felt surges of energy that helped me raise the car another bit and another bit. The bolts were stuck so hard that I didn't think they would come off. But again I asked for help and I was given energy surges. I got the tyre changed.

There was no way that I could have done that by myself.

As I got back on the road it occurred to me that this episode had happened for a reason. In fact, I felt that both occasions of getting a flat tyre within a week had happened for a reason, but I didn't know why.

It became clear a week later when I finally left my job and split with my partner. This was traumatic and frightening and I really believe the angels used the situations to let me know that, no matter what, I was never alone; they would always be there to help me and to give me the courage I needed to get through any serious challenge.

It *is* true, as we've seen; angels can save the day and sometimes change your whole life. It seems that many of these stories are given to me by women who have reached a very low and vulnerable point in their life, when desperation forces them to look for help.

Annie's story

A few years ago a young woman called Annie wrote to me for advice. She was another woman living in a destructive marriage. Her husband was very violent and she was fearful for her safety and that of the children. She was a great believer in God and the angels, but was trapped in the belief that marriage is for ever.

Over the course of a couple of months she frequently emailed me and asked for guidance on how to deal with the situation from a spiritual perspective. She desperately needed to leave with her children and start again. I talked with her about lighting a candle and meditating, affirming that she desired the best possible outcome for all concerned and asking the angels to give her a message that would be unique and meaningful and help her to deal courageously with her situation. Sometimes a white feather is simply not enough proof of divine intervention.

Annie told me how the angels helped her to find the courage she needed to leave a toxic relationship.

I prayed and prayed for help. One morning, after another night of terrible arguments and threatened violence, when I truly felt I could not possibly face my husband again, I took the children down to the park just to get out of the house.

I sat down on a bench close enough to the playground that I could see the children, but far enough away that they could not see me cry. I was so desperate, and still God did not seem to be giving me any answers.

Then a stranger sat down next to me. It was an old lady, scruffily dressed in a tattered black coat, with loads of smelly carrier bags all stuffed full of rubbish. Oh no, I thought. Just my luck. I didn't want anybody to sit with me – not even a bag lady! She turned toward me with a strange toothless grin. There was something a bit odd about her, as well as her clothes and bags, and she made me nervous. But even though I felt I didn't want to encourage her, I couldn't help but smile back. There was warmth about her and when I looked into her eyes they were like deep blue pools.

I didn't say anything to the old lady. I couldn't. So we just sat in silence and I returned to my negative thoughts. Then she spoke to me. She said, "Don't worry, dear, everything will be fine. You will be safe. The children are being protected. You will find the courage you need that you don't think you have. You will turn your life around. You'll see. Please don't cry any more now, dear child."

Then, before I could answer her, she bundled her bags together, stood up and walked away, without even waiting for a reply.

Annie felt puzzled by the stranger's words, as they were so inspirational and meaningful. How on earth, she wondered, could the old woman have known what was going through her mind? She immediately went home, made some telephone calls and sought the assistance of the social services. She packed for herself and the children, and left.

At first she was placed in a safe house, away from her violent husband, and then she found a job, a home and moved away. She has never looked back. She and her children are happy and settled. "The stranger was definitely an angel in disguise," she told me. "As soon as she spoke to me I felt calm and absolutely certain that everything really was going to be all right after all. Somehow she gave me confidence and a deep sense of knowing that I could do anything I put my mind to."

Doreen's story

When another lovely lady from Ireland, Doreen, wrote to me with a similar story, much of it resonated with me and I felt great empathy. Again, the story was about a woman needing courage to change her difficult circumstances and I recognized her fears and challenges – in some ways they closely mirrored some of my own from the past.

While I was growing up, I was drawn to the unusual. Instead of playing with my dolls I walked in the old graveyard or spent my days around the nearby derelict castle, playing. Here I went on magical journeys, through hidden tunnels, seeing mystical creatures and talking to beautiful people. As I grew up my interests changed and I removed myself from the mystical and into the harsh reality that is our world. I forgot all that I had and lived for the moment. I married and had children. My marriage broke down. Although married life was not a pleasant experience, I had my lovely children.

One day I was outside the courthouse during my divorce proceedings, smoking a cigarette to calm my nerves, when a dishevelled woman came up to me. She asked me if she could have a light and when I said she could, she asked me for a cigarette as well! I laughed to myself and thought, "That's a good one, I fell for that easily enough!"

The woman started to talk to me about life, how hard it was and how some men don't make it easy. She looked straight into my eyes and called me by my name and said, "Daughter, you have to stop beating yourself up with that big stick. You carry it around on your back and every so often you give yourself a big slap with it. Carry on and live your life. Do what you are meant to do and don't worry about anyone else."

At that point, my lawyer came outside to call me in. I started up the steps, then I turned to give the woman my cigarettes, but there was no sign of her. She was gone. At the time I did not understand, but her words stuck with me. Now I can look back and understand that this woman was an angel sent to give me courage in my hour of need, when I was at my lowest.

From that moment my quest started. I did not know what or who I was looking for. I found that I had healing gifts and embarked on learning about healing therapies. Years later, with my old skills realigned, I discovered angels. I could feel energies, I could hear them, they took me to wonderful things and on splendid journeys, but still my thirst would not be quenched. I needed spiritual guidance.

I wanted to take Chrissie's course, but couldn't attend classes in person as I live in Northern Ireland. I knew that a home-study course would be perfect for me – and it was. The angels again pointed me in the right direction. I am a very practical person; I ask and I receive. I believe Chrissie was sent, as I asked for someone to guide me and help me understand the journey I was to take. Her teachings gave me an insight that I had not experienced before; she gave me a spiritual awareness that I had been afraid of embracing due to my Catholic upbringing.

Now I use my gifts on a daily basis and I invite angels to assist me to help others. I have never known my angels to fail me.

In all that I do, my angels are with me; my angels are all that I am.

The missionary's story

As a finale for this chapter I would like to tell you another story sent to me demonstrating the power of the angels and their ability to guard us in dire circumstances.

Every two weeks a missionary working in Africa went to the city to purchase medical supplies for the small field hospital where he served. On one of his trips he saw two men fighting in the street. One was seriously injured, so the missionary stopped, treated his wounds and shared God's love with him. Then he headed for home, stopping in the jungle to camp overnight.

When he visited the city two weeks later a man approached him; the same one he'd helped on his previous trip. The man said, "I knew you carried money and medicine with you, so our gang followed you to your camp planning to kill you for the money and the drugs. But, just as we were about to attack, we saw lots of armed guards surrounding you." The missionary replied, "No, that's impossible; I was all alone." The man countered, "But my buddies saw them too. We counted them, there were twenty-six guards."

Months later, when the missionary told this story back at his home church, someone interrupted, "Exactly what day did this take place?" When the missionary identified the specific day, the man was amazed. He said, "On that exact night in Africa it was morning here, and I felt a strange urge to pray for you. It was so strong that I phoned some friends to come to the church and pray with me. Would all of you who prayed with me that day please stand up?" One by one the missionary counted them: the total was twenty-six.

My intention is to offer encouragement to you, the reader, by sharing some of the hard challenges that have been related to me. Whether through prayer or "coincidence", in each story the recipient of the gift of courage has come out of the situation stronger, empowered and inspired, not only physically but emotionally and spiritually, too.

This visualization and meditation enables you to let go of some of the fears in your life. When you do so, the angels will enable you to clear a space for empowerment and courage, if you should need it.

Meditation for Courage

- Sit comfortably in a quiet place, where there are no distractions. Breathe deeply, down into your lower abdomen, and allow your body to relax, starting with your shoulders, neck, face and scalp. As you breathe, continue to relax, imagining you are sinking deeper into your chair.
- Imagine you can see the air changing into your favourite colour and breathe it down into your body, allowing it to fill every cell with beauty and light.
- As you exhale, let go of any tension, discomfort or distractions and simply drift into the loveliness of the light that surrounds you now.
- Now I'd like to take you on a short journey, where you find yourself walking along a beautiful beach. The sky is blue, the air is comfortable and warm, and you are happy to enjoy an empty beach as you stroll along the sea's edge, relishing the warm water caressing your feet. You can feel the sand or pebbles as you walk.

With the sea to your left and land to your right, you are walking toward the light of the sun.

- In the distance you notice someone walking along the edge of the water toward you. This is someone with whom you feel familiar and although you sense the person is very tall you are completely at ease. As you look, you notice the light seems to be shining from above his head and from his face, too, and as you look more closely, also from his heart. Gradually, as the stranger gets closer and closer, you become aware that he is an angel.
- You stop and greet one another. Without words the angel understands your thoughts, your fears and your challenges. He points to the pebbles, where lie various items washed up by the sea. Among them is an old, empty treasure chest.
- The angel indicates that you are to find an object to symbolize your fear, issue or challenge, and place it carefully and lovingly in the box. As you do so, affirm to yourself what object you are placing in the box and what it represents for you. You may do this as many times as necessary, until you feel you have symbolically placed all your fears or worries into the treasure chest.
- Now the angel bends to close the chest and blesses the contents before he takes one handle, and you pick up the other. Together you walk to the edge of the water and place the chest in the sea.
- The angel stands back and, with arms raised, blesses the chest as it begins to float out on the gentle waves, which gradually take it further and further out into

the water. Watch the chest in your mind's eye, until it becomes a mere speck on the horizon. Then the chest disappears. It sinks into the deep ocean, never to be seen again.

- You turn to thank the angel, but find him gone. To your surprise you find there are no footprints in the sand and this amuses you, leaving you with a warm glow in your heart.
- You know that you have completed this act of courage on your own, with the guidance of the angels. You can come back to this beach and repeat the exercise any time you wish.
- Allow yourself to breathe calmly and slowly back into the present moment and give yourself a grounding hug of gratitude for being the special gifted being that you are!

"I am strengthened by the power of unlimited love."

CHAPTER 7

GIFTS OF PEACE

When we are in turmoil within we can simply ask the angels to help us regain composure, and carry on as before. Or we can take time to communicate in silence with Archangel Uriel and the Angels of Peace. To be at peace with the world we must first be at peace with our self. Unity within family groups can develop only when one or more are prepared to let go of the need to be "right". World peace can only ever come from inner peace. Ask the angels to help you to find that inner peace by agreeing to make your corner of the world a little more peaceful.

"Peace, peace, peace, Angel of Peace
be always everywhere."

GOSPEL OF THE ESSENES

Your definitions of "peace" may depend on your life experience. For example, you may instantly think of the peace that comes with cessation of war, or the peace of harmoniously living at one with nature. Then there's that peace that relates to a sense of inner calm, as opposed to anxiety and stress, or that which we find through meditation or prayer. We seek peace if we are in the midst of a cacophony, finding it in stillness and serenity. Then there is the peace brought about by harmonious existence with other beings; or that sense of peace experienced through the passing away of a loved one, especially after a long illness.

Lastly, though most importantly, perhaps, is the peace revered and sought by seekers on their spiritual quest, the kind we call "God's Peace", which "surpasses all understanding".

My peace adventure

Let me start by sharing my adventure with a type of peace that certainly surpassed all my understanding!

My first encounter with the Essenes (see page 15) had been the catalyst that turned my life around. I had been introduced to communion with the angels and found the love and support of a group of people who had quickly become friends. Here I was, returning the following summer, my heart bursting with joy.

I arrived in Yorkshire early for the Essene Summer Gathering. I parked, unloaded my car and set off with my little dog for a walk along the green and peaceful country lanes. It was the middle of August and the sun shone brightly on this glorious English country scene. I was literally skipping for joy. I raised my hands up to heaven in gratitude calling out, "Thank you, thank you, thank you, for all the wonderful changes in my life. Thank you for bringing me back to the Essenes. Here I am. What would you like me to do now?"

I immediately became aware of a tune playing in my head, softly at first and then louder and clearer. I felt that this was a direct response to my question, but couldn't recognize the tune. I listened carefully and hummed the notes, trying to remember where I had heard it before. As I sang the tune quietly under my breath, the words gradually formed in my head and jogged my memory. It was the song "Make Me a Channel of Your Peace". I remembered singing it in Sunday school and it had recently been recorded by the Irish singer, Sinead O'Connor, in tribute to the just-deceased Princess Diana. My jaunty stride became subdued to a slow walk down the hill as I processed the message on my way back to the beautiful old house, where the rest of the members were arriving.

The first person to greet me as I walked toward the house was Anne MacEwen, the president of the organization, taking a stroll under the magnificent trees. I described my experience to her. "I think I understand that I am supposed to be a channel of peace, but how can I do that when I know nothing about politics?" I asked her in all seriousness. "That's fine, dear," she replied with a wry smile. "Why don't you accompany me to Holland for the peace conference next May? You can start your quest for world peace by helping me to distribute the Essene Network literature."

When we arrived at the hall together, several people were drinking tea and chatting. A stranger, whom I later learned was called Patricia, approached us and asked for Christine. "Ah it's you," she said. "How intriguing. I'm to give you this book, which is rather annoying, really, as I am only halfway through it. I was relaxing on my bed reading it when a voice said, 'Go and give this book to Christine; she is one of your group.'" Again I was puzzled, but thanked her, flipping through from back to front. The book was called *Emissary of Peace*, by James Twyman, and as my fingers ran arbitrarily through the pages, I suddenly stopped and began to read.

As I saw the words from the page, a sense of awareness spread through my body like a spine-tingling shudder. The place I had chosen to read was none other than the prayer of St Francis, with its words, "Make me a channel of thy peace" ringing for the second time that day through my head. "Oh my goodness," I realized, "a channel of peace has nothing to do with governments and politics. It's about bringing God's love and harmony. I am here with these people to learn how to do this by working with the angels."

As I stood sipping tea and talking to Patricia, we shared our fascination about how quickly angelic messages from God come through when we are open and receptive. Then the third sign presented itself. Flora, one of our Scottish members, whom I had met the previous year, came over to greet me. We hugged and chatted for a few moments and then she gave me a small gift she had bought earlier, "This is for you," she said smiling. "It has your name on it." It was a beautiful bookmark made from blue ribbon and card with pressed forget-me-nots. In calligraphy in the centre of the bookmark was written, "Lord, make me a channel of your Peace".

The conference in Holland was called "World Peace, Inner Peace". I accompanied Anne and, thanks to her, I met representatives from religious groups from all over the world. I sat around a peace fire with Hopi Native Americans, shared Buddhist meditations and enjoyed enlightening workshops. I heard lectures by highly respected international scientists and religious leaders, was attuned to the overlighting presence of the Archangel Uriel for the first time, and made friends with some wonderfully talented and spiritual people, who have blessed my life.

Gifts from angels

This episode of my life was richly abundant with a wide variety of angelic gifts. The gift of my place at this conference, in particular, was a major inspiration for my studies in comparative religion, teaching and spiritual facilitation, and for my later career and service with the Essenes.

Some of the following stories I have chosen illustrate various experiences of peace, including the passing of a loved one. The passage between worlds and what we call the "loss" of someone dear to us can also be seen by others as a great release. Commonly viewed by atheists as the demise of our earthly existence and the end of life, for those of us who believe in any form of holistic spirituality this is just the beginning of another glorious existence. Those with an understanding of God, angels, reincarnation or the mysterious esoteric teachings of so many religions and cultures may recognize what is called "death" in human terms as the time we make our way back to the Light, or toward other dimensions of existence in other spiritual plains.

But whether we understand death or not, and whether or not our pain is caused by the grief of loss, when we are suffering from deep emotional anguish our soul cries out for comfort. At these times the angels lovingly come closer to us in order to help.

So often, following a cry for help, people experience of a sense of inexplicable calm. This deep calm is then associated with a feeling of inner peace – spiritual peace full of love. It is a gift that is offered to us so generously without conditions, if we wish to accept it.

Here are some of the many moving stories I have received about the gift of peace, and my hope is that they will illustrate just how potent this particular gift can be to the receiver.

Vivian's story

The first is from Vivian, whose baby daughter, Bonnie, was born in April 2006.

At thirty-six years of age Vivian was considered an "older" mum. She was advised to have a series of scans to establish the health and size of the baby and, to her dismay, the doctors noticed that there were some problems. At first they thought her baby had fluid on the brain, but then, when she was eventually born by Caesarean section, there were so many things wrong that Bonnie never left hospital.

She was cared for in hospital for six months and, although she grew in size, there was never enough room for her internal organs to develop properly, and the medical experts decided that no amount of surgery could help. You can imagine that Vivian was devastated when the doctors told her there was nothing more that could be done.

Little Bonnie was taken off all the tubes and placed in my arms. I was given a room and a bed for the night and I just cuddled my baby, waiting for her passing, comforted by my own mother and my boyfriend. I firmly believe that angels appear in that kind of twilight time of semi-consciousness.

As I was lying with Bonnie in my arms, a bright light came into the little room. I saw the room completely fill with light and knew instinctively that an angel was with us, and that the time had come. With a heavy heart I whispered, "Oh please do not take her yet." Then a gentle voice that reminded me of my grandmother said, "But look at Bonnie's little face, she is so happy and peaceful." Through tears flowing down my cheeks of both sadness and relief, I looked down at my baby. Bonnie had passed on. As the bright light faded, I knew in my heart that my much-loved baby daughter had been carried in the arms of an angel to a beautiful heavenly place.

Viv was a wonderful mother while Bonnie was on earth, and she is such a truly loving and special person. Although it still breaks my heart to think that Bonnie has gone, it brings great peace and comfort to know that she is being cared for by the angels. Viv and I are so happy that we are able to share this story with others and we hope they may find some comfort in reading it.

When you carry and lose a baby the emotional pain is truly unbearable. As a parent you never forget the child, who remains locked for ever in your heart. Little Bonnie would have been four years old now, had she lived. Viv had never before, or since, felt so much love for another human being. After she experienced such extremes of anguish and pain, the peace and unconditional love that followed clearly were heavenly gifts to her.

Stephanie's story

Yet not everyone is able to "see" the guiding light of the angels. Without belief or faith in their existence and in God's love, might we miss out on the sense of peace that angelic presence can give to us? Stephanie, another of my course students, wrote to me with that very question.

My sister had been going to the hospital day and night to sit by her husband, who had sustained a massive bleed into his brain and was in a drug-induced coma. I started to go with her toward the end because the hospital had done all that they could to make him comfortable and the prognosis wasn't good.

The time came to switch off the machines that were keeping him alive. My sister just couldn't believe that he wasn't going to make it back to some sort of health and was beside herself with grief. My focus was my sister; their marriage had been volatile and her husband a very difficult man to live with, at times, I think, partly due to the growing tumour in his brain.

It took an hour for his body to relax and take his last breath, by which time my sister was beyond grief. At this point, from my passive viewpoint, I became aware of a bright light that wasn't linked to the hospital's supply and an audible sensation, one so real, so tangible, that I found myself staring at my brother-in-law's now empty body, intrigued.

The feeling of love that was filling the room was so astounding that I looked at my sister to see if she was feeling it, too. But the grief was too immense for her to sense that her husband's angel had come to escort him onward from his pain into another place of love and light.

Then the light and the feeling of love passed and my sister and I were left in an almost darkened room – alone.

I sensed that my sister's grief had blocked out any chance of "feeling" the passing over of her husband and I thought that was so terribly sad, because if she had been able to sense it she would, perhaps, have been at peace and wouldn't have felt her grief so deeply.

It seems to me that there is an unwritten universal law, that, however close or sympathetic we are to our loved ones, we cannot take their pain away, nor can we fully experience the extent of their grief.

Somehow Stephanie's observation of the bright light, seen because she was the witness and not the grieving wife, seems to demonstrate that perhaps, if we were able to embrace death rather than dread it, we would not need to feel such pain. One could also consider that in coming through the pain and finding our way to peace we break through one of humanity's greatest challenges.

The Archangel Gabriel is known as the Angel of Birth and Death, and Azreal has also been given the title of Angel of Death, but just as passing may manifest itself in many forms, so may the Angels of Passing. There is great joy and celebration in birth and there may be such great beauty and joy to celebrate in death. If only more of us could believe that we are actually being born again into a new place of light and a new experience of complete acceptance and love. It is certainly very reassuring and comforting when one reads descriptions of the soul being carried away in the arms of the angels.

Cath's story

So many stories of the Angels of Passing are from the perspective of the relative, but in this next story the observer was the nurse in charge.

My friend Cath has been a nurse all her working life. She firmly believes in angels and has the gift of clairvoyance. Down the years she has told me many wonderful stories and this is one of my favourites.

Cath was ward sister in charge of a busy medical unit, and had contacted a family to advise them of the deteriorating health of their mother. She warned them that they should come to the hospital without delay. The son told Cath that his children were in bed, but they would come as soon as they could find a babysitter.

"I hope Mum will hold on until we arrive, I know she doesn't want to go alone," he told her. Cath assured him that either she or one of the nurses would watch his mother until they arrived.

About twenty minutes later a young girl of around ten years old walked confidently onto the ward toward the room of the patient. Late into the night and expecting no other visitors, Cath approached her, assuming that she could only be the granddaughter of the dying woman.

She greeted her and taking her hand she walked quietly with her into the patient's room.

"If you can sit very quietly, you can wait in here for your mum and dad," Cath said. "Your grandma knows you are here, even though she is very poorly and fast asleep." The girl smiled sweetly in agreement. Cath stood for a while as the girl sat on the chair next to her grandma, then she left them to spend a few moments together, peeking in every now and then to make sure they were all right.

A further twenty minutes passed and suddenly the door to the ward burst open with a very anxious couple rushing in, straight into the sister's office. Cath immediately expressed her surprise at the length of time it had taken them to follow their daughter onto the ward. "I left her sitting with her grandma as I didn't think you would be very long," Cath told them.

They were shocked. Ashen-faced, the young man told Cath that they had only sons. As they all approached the room Cath instinctively knew the patient had already passed over. She had experienced this kind of spiritual phenomenon before, when mysterious "visitors", usually unnoticed by the other staff, arrived on the ward in time for the passing over of one of her patients. Cath had become accustomed to her ability to see clairvoyantly. The visitors always looked as human as anyone else to her.

Sure enough, the girl had disappeared as mysteriously as she had arrived, and their elderly mother was lying still, pain-free, serene and in peace. Was this sweet little girl one of the "guardians of passing"? And did she come to help the loving grandma, who had been devoted to her children, in her transition from one life to the next, escorting her lovingly beyond the veil?

Fred's story

Sometimes the angelic messages are not for personal peace, but for all of humanity. This message about world peace came from the angels through my father, Fred. It caused him quite a dilemma, as you'll understand as you read his story.

Fred has devoted his life to service of a spiritual nature. A healer and mystic for nearly sixty of his eighty years he has learned, through many years of ardent prayer and self-teaching, how to work with Spirit and how to interpret the guidance he receives for himself and for others. He has received many messages through extraordinary visions and paranormal experiences.

This particular strong visual experience was not about his personal spiritual journey, but a message for everyone. It happened quite some time ago on a cold night in the middle of winter.

I was fast asleep when I was woken by a female crossing my bedroom in front of the bed. She was dressed in the clothes of a Victorian housemaid. I immediately recognized her glowing light as that of an angel, in spite of her dress. "My way is better than your way," she said, and she walked past me, through the wall.

Then, as I focused my thoughts, having realized I was not dreaming, she walked back the other way and repeated her statement again while passing through the room: "My way is better than your way." As she re-appeared for the third time and repeated her sentence again, I sat bolt upright in bed. I knew that when things like this happened in threes something important was about to unfold. She had my full attention.

I became aware of a warm, bright light and a profound spiritual presence surrounding me. As my eyes became accustomed to the bright light, I saw that another angel, a male one, was standing in the corner of the bedroom.

This was not a dream, nor was it the first time an angel had woken Fred from his sleep. It had happened many times in his life and he had always received a message. Fred knew that this time he was being given another profound vision.

As I watched carefully images appeared in front of me and, strangely, all around me. It was like a film in 3D was being shown on the bedroom wall – one in which I seemed to be participating. I could see and hear what was happening so clearly, feel it around me. All my senses seemed to be somehow enhanced.

Fred was being shown scenes from an ancient battle.

I had no idea how long ago the battle had taken place, but I could see many men in ancient battledress fighting on foot, with heavy swords. I could smell the horses, watch them rearing, hear the shields and weapons clashing. In those few minutes I watched the fall of many men. I witnessed the bloodshed.

Then the vision stopped. Fred knew that there would be more to come and he waited in anticipation. The next sequence appeared before him, with the same precise clarity. Again he saw many soldiers, but this time they were dressed in the more modern army uniform of World War I.

The soldiers were marching steadily along a long, dusty road. Many were wounded and limping or supported by others. They all looked dishevelled and were clearly battered, beaten and worn down. But all these soldiers were singing as they tried to march in step, "It's a long way to Tipperary, it's a long way from home...". I seemed to know that this old war song was more profound than I had ever thought it before. I couldn't quite work out why, but then as I watched this vision, I began to understood that the word "home" meant heaven... and that war itself was a far distant cry from any divine plan of God's.

Fred also knew that in all his messages there has been a sequence of three, and so he waited for the final part, the third vision. Then it came. The third in the sequence brought with it an eerie silence.

I could see a vision of such incredible natural beauty that it caught my breath and disturbed me more deeply than I could at first understand. It was like searing pain deep down, within my heart. I was being shown magnificent views, wonderful high mountains and glistening lakes, majestic trees and rolling meadows... such beautiful countryside all around me, but my heart was breaking. I could see all the things I hold dear about the world; my own home surroundings, here in the Lake District. Yet I felt unbearable pain and immense sadness that are almost indescribable now.

There was something strange about this vision, something unusual.

This time the colours were different; they looked unnatural. The sky was copper coloured. At first I thought I was being shown a picture in sepia, as it was almost like an old-fashioned photograph. Then the realization hit me. I knew what was missing. There was not a single movement. All was silent. There wasn't a flutter of a wing, nor any sound of birdsong. There were no people. No animals. There was no sign of life.

And again, in that instant, a deep inner knowing and realization hit him. Fred knew that this third vision was of a time in the future. He was being shown a world that no longer contained any human or animal life. His angel guides were giving him a clear view of a possible future in which the world that had suffered a terrible man-made disaster – a disaster of catastrophic proportions that would eradicate all life. His third vision was showing Fred the aftermath of nuclear war. He was overwhelmed and confused by what he had seen.

Then, to his surprise, Fred found himself staring into the sky.

It had started to snow. Big beautiful snowflakes seemed to be falling fast in front of my eyes. Faster and faster they fell, everywhere. But as I watched closely I saw that they weren't snowflakes at all. Millions of pieces of white paper were raining down to the earth from the heavens.

And I could see what they were. Miraculously – as if each piece of paper was speaking to me – I could tell that they all had writing on them. I could read every one of the millions of snowflake-sized pieces of paper, all at the same time. They were all pieces torn from pages of the Gospels of the Holy Bible. They were the words of the parables of Jesus and they all contained the same quotation, "Love one another, as I have loved you."

As the vision faded Fred began to process its meaning and allow it to settle into his understanding. But he was not alone. To his delight and surprise the angel standing in the corner of the room began to sing the words of an old song.

He had the most glorious tenor voice and sang as clearly and as beautifully as you would expect any angel to sing. When he had finished, the angel sang the song again, and then again; he sang it three times from start to finish.

At first, Fred just listened, appreciating the melody and the beauty of the voice, but with a growing knowledge that, like everything else in the vision, the words of the song played an important role in the overall message. The first time he listened, he recognized the lyrics of "Ah Sweet Mystery of Life", an old song that had been very popular in his youth. The second time, he heard the lyrics' deeper meaning.

And the third time I heard the angel sing, the words pierced me like a bolt through the heart. It was almost painful, as if every cell in my body was hit by realization at the same moment:

"For 'tis love, and love alone, the world is seeking."

Fred sat up through the rest of the night. He knew it was not going to be easy to tell anyone about his experience, yet clearly the purpose of the vision was to spread this message of the angels to as many people as he could. And so, in answer to his prayers and meditation, with the guidance of his angels, he came up with the idea of making tapes of the song and giving them to everyone he knew, especially to those who believed in visions and divine messages.

It was a very difficult challenge. No music shop had copies of this old song, and without today's access to the internet he could find no recordings of it or even trace the sheet music. Fred asked for further guidance from his angels and in response had an idea. He visited an office of the BBC in Carlisle, where a kind young researcher could give him a tape with three versions of the song.

It is a very beautiful old song. To many it seems an ordinary love song, yet the message is loud and clear. We must all return to love. Before we make the wrong choices, before it is too late, we must learn to treat one another and our beautiful planet that is our home with universal love and respect.

This miraculous story of Fred's angelic intervention occurred in Fred's twilight years. Spending over half a century mentoring, healing people and countless sick animals, he has also saved many a soul from despair with his wonderful sense of humour and kindness. Fred's passion for life comes from his knowledge and experience of the power of God's love, which, since his visitation, he enjoys sharing. It is his finely tuned connection with the angels and heavenly realms that has guided him through much of his life.

An accident

Fred still felt that he had a good few years of active service left in him but that expectation was to be challenged when he was enjoying a walk early one evening. As he crossed the market square of a busy Lakeland town, a van reversed straight into him, knocking him over and hitting his head, hard. An ambulance was called, his wife and other daughter were sent for, and he was rushed into a Newcastle hospital for assessment. A large blood clot was found to be forming in his brain. This was serious and so, without delay, I drove, with my son, the hundreds of miles to be by his side. Fearing the worst, I sent a prayer to the angels. After a smooth journey we finally caught sight of the great Angel of the North sculpture, arriving in Newcastle by early light.

We learned that a chest X-ray had showed signs of infection. Considering this and his age, it was feared that an operation would be too dangerous, so doctors agreed to wait and allow the clot to dissolve in its own time. Fred was pleased to see us and taking my hand tightly he whispered, "I have been given signs from the angels telling me something else is wrong. There are two things, Chris. They are telling me it is serious."

In extreme pain, he couldn't work the second problem might be, and trusted that it must be a type of pneumonia. Stoically, he rallied at the sight of his grandson. After consultations with doctors it was decided that he would be given pain relief and bed rest, to allow him to recover gradually. Fred seemed to understand that we were not staying. Thanking us for coming to see him, he reassured me that his angels whispered, "Everything is being taken care of." With smiles and relief, my son and I set off back down the long road to London.

Emergency operation

Within a few hours Fred's condition had deteriorated so rapidly that an emergency operation was arranged. Fred spent five and a half hours in theatre undergoing brain surgery. This frightening news forced me to drop my son in London and head back to Newcastle.

Days of intensive nursing began. It was so hard to watch the strong, cheerful Fred being fed by tube and in need of constant pain relief. Fred remained calm and his nurses grew to love his positive attitude. Although he seemed to be sleeping, Fred was in constant prayer and his "angel signs" came through with guidance. Sometimes the signs told him that the situation was very serious and could turn either way, but usually they said that if he worked hard at recovery all would be well. He knew he must rest and, with incredible resilience to the pain, he tried to do so. Intuitively he knew he should exercise his legs and feet, senses and mind whenever possible.

The power of the love he had so often talked about was shining in Fred as he lay in bed. His wife and two daughters kept vigil, giving our energy, love and constant encouragement. We spoke to him of all the friends who were sending good wishes, and read him the messages that had come in from all over the country. We told him how much we loved him, and how hundreds of others were sending love and healing energy through our presence each day.

A visualization

During one quiet session of healing prayer, having been left alone with him for a few moments, I asked the angels to show themselves around his bed. I called upon the Archangel Raphael. Then as I sat in meditative prayer I visualized, and felt, the impressions of four large beings, one on each side of the bed, a third at Fred's feet and a fourth at his head. There was a light circling Fred's head that spiralled down through the ceiling, shaped like a tornado of light. It was very emotional. I had the sense that the light was communicating with him and for a few seconds felt that I understood the meaning of his "signs". I sensed the angels whispering to him, giving him instructions: "Think of happy memories, blue skies and rainbows to keep your pain under control. Counting and observing all the technical equipment around the bed will stimulate your mind."

"You are in good hands, the angels are with you," I told him. Then, noticing the nurse's name badge as she returned, I whispered, "Even your nurse is called Angela."

Each day his inner signs from the angels told him what to do next.

His constant struggle to remember his full name, where he was and when he was born caused him great amusement and it was his incredible cheerfulness and sense of humour in practising the same questions, hour upon hour, that impressed the staff.

Gradual recovery

Very soon he was out of intensive care and into the high-dependency unit. Within a few days he was sitting in a chair, eating and trying to stand. His angels still warned him that he wasn't out of danger, but said that with rest and careful management he would recover. His family brought him nutritious foods and drinks and special treats, and together we gave him reflexology for his hands and feet, and took turns in holding his hands when he was sleeping.

Suddenly, his signs changed and Fred was warned that all was not well. The angels told him that the constant use of the oxygen mask was not right for him and might weaken him, yet he could not breathe without it. As the eldest daughter and first to arrive on the ward that day I was asked to make uncomfortable decisions about his care, and whether we would like to put Fred onto a ventilator. The time was approaching when he would no longer be able to breathe without assistance. It was extremely distressing.

When I gently explained to Fred what he might need to consider he quietly asked for angelic guidance. The immediate response was, "Yes, there is a serious problem that needs urgent attention. All will be well. That decision will not be necessary!"

A little later, as Fred sat up, struggling for breath, my attention was drawn to his swollen stomach. For someone who had been unable to eat for several days, this was unusual weight gain. I felt that he had accumulated fluid around his stomach and called the staff. A prompt scan showed massive quantities of fluid, which needed to be removed. Afterwards Fred could immediately breathe again without the aid of oxygen, and he could enjoy his dinner in comfort.

Fred's recovery after that was amazing. Within a few weeks he was back in his local hospital for rest and recuperation, strengthening his walking and improving his speech. Conversation, including memory skills, slowly returned and he was sent home.

This is a story with an apparently happy ending, but it is part of a bigger picture and the outcome is broader than it seems at first.

Finding meaning

Fred pondered endlessly on the events of the accident. He had set off on a gentle stroll on a pleasant evening. His life had been dedicated to God's work, the loving and essential message of Jesus, and the sharing of healing with those in need. He had felt there was still so much to do, that as time was speeding up for him, his mission was becoming even more urgent, and vital. Then why was he suddenly knocked off his feet?

The first part of the answer came to me in a flash of inspiration during one of my long drives to and from the hospital – I had many hours for contemplation. I have often spent my driving hours in conversation with God. In more recent years I have included communication with the angels and I am forever asking questions, which are sometimes answered. Other times I have to work the answers out for myself. On this occasion the angels answered straight into my thoughts.

"This accident and the recovery is a living example of the healing power of the angels through pure unconditional love." Of course. I had known that – but sometimes words are inadequate.

The power of three

Everyone who knew and loved Fred and his wife sent their love and healing energy through her unconditional love. Everyone who knew and loved his youngest daughter sent their love and healing energy through her unconditional love. Everyone who knew about Fred's accident and who knew and loved me, his eldest daughter, sent their love and healing energy through my unconditional love.

When the love of so many is channelled through three people in this way it triples the effect. This is the power and the magic of the mystical number three. The intention of three sets up a triangle, which is so often used in prayer. The reason why prayers and fiats to the angels are repeated three times is because this number contains the essence of the spiritual mystery of the Trinity.

Even more miraculous than this proof of the power of love is the synchronicity of the accident. We learned after Fred's surgery that there had been a burst blood vessel in his brain that may have been slowly bleeding for weeks. It would have been one of many thinning blood vessels, probably caused by a decade of medication, which simply burst and caused a bleed – and would undoubtedly have caused Fred to have another massive stroke. The blood clot caused by the accident was directly on top of the bleed and, by adding pressure, it temporarily arrested the bleed, which was discovered during the brain surgery and could be halted.

The accident happened almost ten years to the day since Fred had his previous stroke. This one would more than likely have been fatal because of his age. The massive blood clot of the haemorrhage actually saved Fred's life.

Through what can only be divine intervention on that fateful Thursday afternoon, Fred's life was saved when a driver knocked him over. And this miraculous story of recovery was to create, through Fred, a living example of the power of love.

Sylvia's story

Gifts from the angels are not always given as a dream-like vision or whispered message; they can be visible signs in a physical form. This is a lovely story from Sylvia, who has seen many angels throughout her eighty years. She shares her first clear angel memory here.

I have been blessed with seeing or feeling angelic presence since a child. As a tiny child I would play amongst my "invisible" garden elvin friends, but my very first experience of actually seeing an angel was when I was around seven or eight years old.

My mother had been rushed into hospital after a serious accident. While pregnant, she had fallen down a flight of stone steps and miscarried, losing her child. I went with my distraught father to the hospital and, as children were not allowed onto the wards in the 1930s, I sat in the corridor twisting my dress out of shape and watching through the open door.

The ward sister had tried to comfort me, with little success, but agreed to leave the door open so that I could see down the long ward past all the other beds to my mother's, where my father sat.

As I gazed through the doors down to my mother's bed, I saw a beautiful lady standing there, dressed in a nurse's uniform that was different from all the others, a lovely shade of light blue. She was gently stroking my mother's head, looking at her so lovingly as she whispered something to her. I gazed, bewildered, wondering what she was saying, until – as another nurse approached – the lady in blue turned to look directly at me, then held her finger to her lips as if to say "shush", it was to be a secret.

Then the lady in blue disappeared. I asked my father later who she had been. He hadn't seen her at all and smiled quizzically at me as if this were another of my fanciful notions.

I just knew, then, that the lady was an angel, looking after my mother, and that she would soon get well and come home. I felt totally reassured and even though I was so young I was at peace with the situation.

This was my first experience of the love and reassurance of our guardian angels, something I would learn even more profoundly throughout the rest of my life.

Tracey's story

Sometimes, when the angels visit us, they leave behind a physical sign. Here is one of many accounts of the inexplicable appearance of feathers. Many of us believe that feathers are a sign of angelic presence. This is not because the feathers come from the wing of an angel, but because these little white birds' feathers appear so often in such unlikely places and circumstances that they have taken on the symbolic meaning of a "message from the angels".

This is how Tracey began to believe in angels.

I'm going back a few years now, to when my elderly grandma was unfortunately admitted to hospital. Her health wasn't great and she deteriorated quite rapidly after admission. She kept having these turns when the family was contacted to go to the hospital as they thought she was about to die.

On one of these occasions, we were gathering in the hospital's family room. The doctors and nurses were with my grandma and we were told she wouldn't make it. As you can imagine, we were all upset, but then the nurse entered the room and said she had pulled through and was now comfortable.

We all gathered around my grandma's bedside, and she was quite alert and smiling and talking to us. The nurse then came to us and explained that while my grandma was "out of it", a single white feather had floated down and landed on her. She said that they didn't use feathers in any of their bedding and wouldn't have them anywhere in the hospital as they're an irritant to patients who have certain allergies.

The nurse had kept the feather, which my aunty still has. My grandma died about a week later and I believe this was her angel giving her a little bit more time with her family, to say goodbye.

I miss my grandma terribly, but when she left this world she gave me with a special, beautiful gift – a belief in angels. I have been reading and learning about angels ever since, and I know they are with me all the time, caring, guiding and protecting me.

Feathers are frequently described by people as confirmation of angelic presence. I also like to think of them as affirmations or signs that wherever we are, or whatever we are thinking, in that moment we are being blessed by the angels.

Angie and Sami's story

Angie is a nurse whose love of angels led her to contact me. She wrote to me with a very beautiful and moving tribute to her daughter, whom she believes was (and is) an angel, because she brought such love to everyone she met during her nineteen years on earth.

As a child Sami had an accident, falling from a friend's bedroom window. She sustained head injuries that left her in a coma for four weeks, before recovering in hospital. During that time she was unable to speak. Months later, when she had recovered her speech a little, she told her mother how she was missing her friends from hospital. This was a mystery because only her immediate family and one or two school friends had been to her bedside.

Sami showed her mother pictures she had drawn to describe her visitors. To Angie's amazement the beautiful pictures showed Sami surrounded by fifteen or twenty angels. "Who are these people?" Angie asked. "These are my friends," Sami explained. She said that they had been with her all the time in hospital. They would hum long soothing notes, but they did not have mouths.

She told me that they talked to her with their minds. I was astonished, intrigued, shocked, thrilled, grateful – so many emotions. She also said she could often sit up and watch Simon, her brother, and me as we sat next to her, looking so sad that she wanted to touch us. She also wanted to say "Mummy" but couldn't. She said she never felt afraid, and when she came home, one angel came with her and would always twinkle near her head.

Sami went on to make an amazing recovery and grew up to be a clever, compassionate, loving and caring young woman. She returned to school and excelled in all her studies, bringing joy wherever she went.

Sami was accepted into university to study dentistry and I was so very proud of her. On the Mother's Day that year I received the most moving card from Sami, telling me how much she loved me. It was almost like a goodbye.

Then on the night of the 18 March, after a long chat on the phone when she told me again how much she loved me, and had the same conversation with her little sister, I had a dreadful dream in which Sami was killed by a bus.

In my dream it was dark. I saw a blue double-decker bus, then I only heard noises – a bang, then the screech of brakes, over and over again. I woke myself up, got a drink, wandered about, then went back to bed. I was immediately taken back to this dream. I tried to approach the bus to find out what it was telling me, but there was no driver, the lights were off downstairs and I couldn't see any passengers. I walked up the stairs. The light was on and in the aisle was the body of a woman wearing jeans and trainers. I thought, "Is it Sami? Is it me?" There was a baby blanket covering the woman's torso and head, soaked in blood. I tried to pull the blanket off, but every time I removed it another one was in its place.

I felt the dream was a premonition and that it could be about me, as I had to drive to Oxford to attend a course. I was very uneasy and tried to contact Sami the next morning, but couldn't. The day started in its normal frantic way of getting my younger daughter Fae up and ready for school. I drove down to Oxford to do my course.

I had a bad feeling all day. When I got home, a policeman was waiting. He said that Sami had been killed on a pedestrian crossing. The traffic had been stationary but, as she crossed, a bus overtook and hit her, killing her instantly. Sami died at nineteen minutes to nine, on 19 March 1999, and she was nineteen years old.

Anyone interested in numerology will find the significance of these numbers fascinating, as the number nine signifies completion. In her email, Angie also told me:

I know Sami is an angel looking out for me. I have so many stories about the help I receive from her. For example, the latest was when I made a decision to change my car. It was a T-reg, ancient thing and falling apart, and as I was discussing my problem with my son, who now lives in the USA, he told me about car leasing. The next day I saw an advert in the paper – a local garage was doing just that. I found this lovely little car, but I wasn't sure I could manage the payments, so I told the salesman I was just going to pop home and talk to my daughter. I went home, sat quietly and said "Sami, my angel, if this is the right thing to do give me a sign."

I went back to the garage and the salesman asked where my daughter was. I gingerly told him that she was in heaven, but she would leave me a sign, usually a white feather, if I was making the right decision. He looked at me in a strange way and we walked around to the back of the forecourt to where the car was. We approached the driver's side first and there we saw six pure-white feathers on the seat. Then we walked around to the passenger side, where there were about twenty feathers. The salesman was squealing and said he had to ring his wife to tell her!

Angie finished her email to me with these words:

"I think the amount we grieve for Sami matches the amount we loved her. We are better people for knowing her, and we had fourteen extra years with her after her fall. At the funeral I was given a book with angels on the

cover. Inside, all her friends, teachers, even people who had just met Sami once had written about how she'd had an impact on their lives and changed them for ever. I know she was an angel.

A medium friend told me that she is now welcoming children into heaven when they feel lost or frightened, and I feel such peace knowing that she sends me beautiful butterflies and feathers as signs that she is still around.

Kate's story

It is very hard to follow such a moving story, but here's another lovely example of the peace and comfort brought to us by angelic signs. This story comes from one of my students, Kate, in Ireland.

I was keeping an eye on my sister's three girls, Ellen (nine), Erin (eight) and Eve (six), and on my own two children, Emily (eight) and Thomas (five), while she ran an errand. It was such a beautiful day, the sun was shining and the children were playing in the back garden.

I took the newspaper out to the picnic table to read and watch the children play, enjoying the late-afternoon sun. As I watched them all together I began thinking of my daddy, who had sat at the same place almost four years ago watching a very similar scene with the children, just about a week before his sudden death aged fifty-nine. Suddenly a breeze blew loads of tiny white feathers into the garden at the very moment I had been thanking God and his angels for the happy scene before me. It really made me happy and grateful for the little things we see and are able to enjoy while we are alive, and great peace of mind at the notion of my dad sharing it with me.

Physical evidence

Feathers and orbs are creating much excitement as increasing numbers of people collect physical evidence of spiritual presence.

On a recent trip to Ireland I was quite amazed by one of the younger members of the audience at a talk I was giving in County Carlow. During the talk and meditation one particular young lady was seemingly distracted and unable to keep her eyes closed during the guided visualization. As the facilitator, I noticed her behaviour and wondered if perhaps she was uncomfortable, or if the evening was not to her liking. In the interval she took the opportunity to come straight over to me and asked if I would mind stepping outside, beyond earshot of the others.

"Who is that standing with you as you are talking?" she asked me. "As soon as you started there was a figure by your side, and as you went into the guided visualization it went behind you and grew into a huge white light that seemed to kind of bend over you."

I readily admitted that, although I often feel a presence, I rarely see anything with my physical eyes. "And another thing," she went on excitedly, "in the corner, over to the left, I could see three balls of light moving around those people there." I explained that some people believe the orbs to be angels, and others consider them spiritual energy, but that we don't actually know whether they represent the spirit of those who have passed over, or true angelic spirit form.

Later, during the question-and-answer session, it transpired that three people who were sitting where the orbs had been seen had very recently lost a loved one. With their permission we were then able to discuss openly whether the orbs could be the spirits of those who had passed, or angel guardians of peace for the ones who were grieving. Either way it was a beautiful experience for everyone concerned.

Julie's story

Finally, in my last story, we can see how animals, especially "man's best friend", can bring angelic comfort. Here's Julie's story:

I'll start at the beginning. I went through a rather messy divorce in 1995 and my two small boys and I were presented with a wonderful present from my sister: a male Golden Labrador Retriever puppy, whom we named Beano. Beano became my shoulder to cry on and my silent counsellor, and gave love to all three of us unconditionally. By 1998 I had met a wonderful man who adored Beanie as much as the three of us did, and in September 2003 Beanie became the "best man" at our wedding, along with filling the roles of my husband's assistant chef and chief security officer!

In the autumn of that same year, we decided to get a companion for him: a male Rhodesian Ridgeback puppy, whom we called Reggie. Beanie was gentle, loving and protective and became Reggie's hero. By 2006 Beanie was showing signs of arthritis and we put him on medication to ease his discomfort, but by the autumn of 2007 he was deteriorating at an alarming rate and despite several visits to our marvellous vet he just wasn't getting any better.

One very frosty autumn evening, when my husband was away on business, I let Beanie and Reggie out for their nightly patrol and after calling and calling found Beanie collapsed – his legs just wouldn't hold him any more. Every morning during the next week we dragged his bed to the back door and then held his body up for him whenever he needed to pee; it was heartbreaking. We decided, after long consultations with our vet and much soul-searching, that the kindest thing we could do for him was to have him put to sleep.

I spent the next few days praying as I have never prayed before that the angels would take him in his sleep so that he would not have to face the trauma of a lethal injection. About three days before the arranged date, a couple of strange things happened. One afternoon Reggie lay down with his head against Beanie's head and rubbed up and down gently – something he had never done before. He then got up, walked away and lay down on his own.

That same night I woke up with a jolt, swung around in bed and saw what I can only describe as the outline of an angel with wings outstretched, looking similar to a photographic negative. It was floating about 1ft off the ground and was about 5ft tall. Now, I am the biggest scaredy cat when it comes to anything at night and I hate the dark, but I just sat up in bed with the biggest grin on my face and I remember saying out loud, "It's an angel". It stayed for about ten seconds, then faded.

We all decided that Beanie should have the dignity and comfort of dying in his own bed, in his own home. The night before he was put to sleep I could not sleep at all and was still begging the angels to take him in the night. As I lay in bed I saw in the corner of the room a ball of sparkling light. It was just hovering at ceiling level and didn't move.

As I lay there, in my head I was pleading, "Please don't go". Although I didn't know what it was, I wasn't afraid. The ball of light stayed there for well over an hour and then gradually faded.

Then something else happened. Just above the edge of the duvet that was covering myself and my husband, a vivid jade-green light appeared like a solid wave on the sea, moving really slowly. I can remember whispering to myself, "What the hell is that?" I am ashamed to say that at the time I was really frightened, because it was just too much – although now I wish I'd had the courage to look over the top of the duvet and see what was in the bedroom. I am convinced that it was Archangel Raphael, bringing healing and comfort for the day ahead.

On 28 November 2007 Beanie was put to sleep. He knew that it was his time to go and his tail kept wagging to the end as we cradled him in our arms and said, "Goodnight, sweet dreams." After our vet had left and Beanie had gone I felt something cold and soft brush against my hand: he said goodbye and then the angels carried him home.

The strange thing was that Reggie completely ignored everything, although he was in the same room. It was as if he had already said his goodbyes that afternoon when he lay down with Beanie. And amazingly, I, who hadn't known how I was going to hold it together for Beanie and the rest of the family, was emotionally in control until the end.

I thank the angels for giving me strength. Although they didn't take Beanie in his sleep, they did answer my prayers, for I think he needed us to be with him as he left this world, to return home.

Although we will never forget Beanie, we now have a wonderful new addition to our family. Her name is Bunty, named in honour of Beano. She is a Goldendoodle and a joy; she has brought new life to Reggie and to our home.

I have found great comfort in knowing that, when we need them the most, the angels let us know that they are always here for us, with their never-ending love, peace, protection and healing.

There are many ways to connect with peace. As we know, some people regularly spend time praying for world peace and actively send energy and white light to areas where there is conflict. However, my experience at the peace conference taught me that, to be of service to the greater cause, we first have to work on finding peace within ourselves.

Here is a meditation for peace, invoking the great Archangel Uriel and the Angels of Peace.

Meditation for Peace

- Sit comfortably in your own quiet place, with your spine straight and your hands open, palms upward and resting in your lap. Breathe slowly and deeply.
- Imagine that around you is a circle of golden light. Bright, rich, golden light that gleams and shines as the circle slowly spins around your feet, slowly rising and spinning around your body, until it rises above your head, then slowly comes down again and rests at heart level. See the light as it spins around you, embracing and protecting you in angelic golden light.
- Call to your own guardian angels and ask them to come close to you now. Feel the warmth of their love

surrounding you as they approach and enter your auric field of energy.

- Visualize a beautiful rich, red colour and call upon the mighty presence of the Archangel Uriel. In this presence accept and allow yourself to feel the peace within your body. Let go, now, of all tension in your muscles and feel the presence of peace in your feet... in your legs... in your hips... in your back... in your stomach... in your chest... in your shoulders... in your arms... in your hands... in your neck... in your face... in your head and scalp.
- Allow yourself to feel completely relaxed now. Visualize the golden circle shining as stars before you.
- Imagine that you can hear the gentle music of the spheres ringing in your ears. You may even feel a tingling of the scalp and an opening of the third eye. Your body and your senses are harmonizing with the whole universe.
- You are connecting with the universal energy of God's peace, the peace that surpasses all understanding. If you feel you would like to offer yourself in service to universal peace and you are ready to work with the Angels of Peace, offer this now: "Archangel Uriel and the Angels of Peace, I am ready to be at peace. I am ready to feel peace in my body, peace in my mind, peace in my heart, peace in my spirit, peace in my soul. I offer myself now as a channel of peace. Use me as a messenger of God's peace."
- Now, breathing in the beautiful rich, red light that surrounds you, sense the gentle, slow movement of the circle of golden light as it spins around your body.

First the circle of light passes down to your feet as if melding with the earth energies, then it rises slowly up your body, strengthening your spine as it goes, giving you purpose and fortitude, stamina and stability. The golden circle of light rises high above your head as you watch it in your mind's eye. It passes through the ceiling, the roof, out into the sky and continues upward. Watch it in your imagination as it moves slowly through the clouds, upward toward the stars.

- Imagine yourself floating with the circle of golden light, surrounded and supported by the Angels of Peace. The golden circle has now formed a beautiful golden bubble of light. The angels take positions around it and pull, bursting the bubble and sending sparkles of loving peace back down toward the earth, landing wherever you feel peace and love are needed.
- As the angels escort you back down to where you are now sitting you feel energized, safe, fully supported by the universe, God and the angels. You feel totally and completely at peace.
- Sitting and breathing slowly, begin to ground your energy back into your body, with your feet flat on the floor and your hands on your lap. Squeeze your fingers and wriggle your toes. Breathe into your "hara", your lower abdomen. When you are ready, slowly and kindly open your eyes.

"I exalt the Divine within as I accept the gift of true spiritual peace."

Further Reading

If you enjoyed reading about angels and would like to know more, I recommend the following:

Chrissie Astell, *Advice from Angels: Messages from the Angels We Meet Every Day*, Godsfield: London, 2005

The Angel Insight Pack: Oracle Cards for Inspiration, Guidance and Wisdom, Duncan Baird Publishers: London, 2008

Discovering Angels: Wisdom, Healing, Destiny, Duncan Baird Publishers: London, 2005

Glennyce S. Eckersley, *Saved by the Angels: True Stories of Angels and Near-death Experiences*, Rider: London, 2002

Glennyce S. Eckersley and Gary Quinn, *An Angel Forever: How to Keep an Angelic Presence with You Throughout Your Life*, Rider: London, 2005

Karen Goldman, *The Angel Book: A Handbook for Aspiring Angels*, Simon & Schuster: London, 1992
This was one of the first "angel" books I read and contains a delightful selection of inspirational suggestions for all would-be angels out there.

Rosemary Ellen Guiley, *Ask the Angels: Bring Angelic Wisdom into Your Life*, Element: London, 2003
This guide to bringing angelic wisdom into your life is written in a beautiful "down-to-earth" manner that I thoroughly enjoyed.

Emma Heathcote-James, *Seeing Angels: True Contemporary Accounts of Hundreds of Angelic Experiences*, John Blake Books: London, 2002
These true-life encounters were the basis of a BBC Everyman documentary.

Anne MacEwen, *Stepping Stones to a New Understanding: A Personal Exploration*, Englang Publishing: Cirencester, 1991
A beautiful introduction to the Angel Communions written by the Essenes and translated from texts found in the Dead Sea Scrolls.

Carmel Reilly, *Walking with Angels: Inspirational Stories of Heavenly Encounters*, Silverdale Books: Leicester, 2005

More true stories of encounters with the angels.

Jenny Smedley, *Soul Angels*, Hay House: London, 2010

My Angel Diary 2012, Hay House: London, 2011
Both book and diary provide a warm and simple way of connecting to the angels.

Doreen Virtue, *Daily Guidance from your Angels: Oracle Cards*, Hay House: London, 2006
365 inspiring messages, one for each day of the year.

Books by contributors

The many excellent books on angels written by contributors to this book include the following:

Ishvara d'Angelo, *Angels in our Time: Why They're Here, How to See Them and How to Work with Them*, O Books: Ropley, 2006

William Bloom, *The Endorphin Effect: A Breakthrough Strategy for Holistic Health and Spiritual Wellbeing*, Piatkus: London, 2001

Working with Angels, Fairies and Nature Spirits, Piatkus: London, 1998

Theolyn Cortens, *The Angels' Script: The Power of the Archangels at Your Fingertips*, Soul School Publishing: 2004 (box-set edition, with cards)

Living with Angels: Bringing Angels into Your Everyday Life, Piatkus: London, 2003

2012: The Teachings of the Nephalim, O Books: Ropley, 2011

Working with Archangels: A Path to Transformation and Power, Piatkus: London, 2007

Working with Your Guardian Angel: An Inspirational 12-week Programme for Finding Your Life's Purpose, Piatkus: London, 2005

Your Guardian Angel Needs You! How to Step into a Remarkable Future, Piatkus: London, 2011

Jacky Newcomb, *Angel Secrets: Transform Your Life with Guidance from Your Angels*, Godsfield: London, 2010

Dear Angel Lady: Amazing True Stories about the Afterlife, Hay House: London, 2009

Aidan Storey, *Angels of Divine Light*, Transworld Ireland: Dublin, 2009

Resources

Chrissie Astell offers a comprehensive seven-part home-study course and a diploma in facilitation, as well as her workshops, one-to-one consultations and various meditation CDs. Find out more at www.angellight.co.uk and www.educatingheartandsoul.com.

To accompany this book there is a dedicated website, www.giftsfromangels.info, for enquiries and sharing stories of your own (see page 226 for more details).

For more information about "angel authors" who have kindly contributed their stories, please visit their websites:

Ishvara d'Angelo makes exquisite angel paintings. She also paints fairies and elves, sculpts and is a published author.
www.angelart.me.uk

William Bloom is the author of many books and one of the UK's leading teachers and authors in the field of spiritual and holistic development.
www.williambloom.com

Theolyn Cortens is the author of a series of excellent angel books. She also offers home study and eClasses, a diploma for teachers and training in Shefa, a unique spiritual technology for awakening our highest potential.
www.theolyn.com

Mark Hughes, singer-songwriter, is famous for his beautiful "The Angel Song" and is the composer of *On the Wings of Angels*, the meditation CD by Chrissie Astell.
www.markhughesmusic.com

Darren Linton channels inspiring messages and teaches people how to connect with their angels and spirit guides. www.guidedbyangels.info

Jacky Newcomb, "The Angel Lady", is the author of several books specializing in paranormal and angel experiences. www.jackynewcomb.com

Aidan Storey works in Ireland as a leading psychic, Angel Therapy Practitioner®, angel reader and author. www.angelicireland.com

Other recommended websites

The Essene Network International
This network seeks to re-establish closer cooperation with the angels in accordance with the Dead Sea Scrolls.
www.essenenetwork.org

Fountain
This is a worldwide community-healing project based on the simple concept that communities, like people, suffer from dis-ease and may be healed.
www.fountain-international.org

Triangles
Part of a worldwide organization encouraging the power of prayer in groups of three participants.
www.triangles.org

Wrekin Trust
An educational charity started in 1971 by Sir George Trevelyan for spiritual education of a non-sectarian kind.
www.wrekintrust.org

www.giftsfromangels.info

Gifts from Angels has a dedicated website where you can receive and interpret your own angelic gifts. You can download free visualizations guided by Chrissie, along with her angel interpretations, guidance and wisdom, and take part yourself by submitting your own stories of angelic encounters and amazing experiences – Chrissie wants to hear from you, too!

During her workshops and talks, Chrissie often takes people on a journey to meet their personal angels. In the meditative presence of these beautiful beneficent beings, her students are given gifts. These may be a feeling or sensation, such as love or serenity, a spoken word or a tangible object. In "The Seven Doors" meditation, Chrissie guides you to a place where you'll receive seven gifts from angels – perhaps symbols of divine guidance, healing or comfort. You can listen to "The Seven Doors" and participate free at the website.

Message from Chrissie Astell

Over the years that I have been facilitating workshops I have found that many people are given the same gifts from the angels in their guided visualizations. It would seem that the recipient is often awakening to a spiritual call and about to embark on the next stage of a spiritual awareness. There are so many moments of recognition on the faces of the participants, once an explanation is given. I believe the gifts are meant to be a clue for spiritual destination, or a symbolic initiation into the next stage of development. It is up to the individual to be ready to accept the guidance, so freely given.

Join Chrissie and discover more about
Gifts From Angels at:
www.giftsfromangels.info

Acknowledgments

Firstly, thank you to all the friendly people at DBP who have worked with me and encouraged me over recent years, especially Bob.

This line of work brings abundant treasure in the form of many interesting and wonderful experiences and people. So many influential people have come into, or passed through, stages of my life, far too many to mention all by name, but they all know who they are, and I thank them whole-heartedly for the gifts they have shared with me.

But how could I have ever moved this far in my work and books about the wonder of angelic gifts, without the amazing and loving support of *all* my friends, family, students, readers and many teachers?

Immeasurable thanks for the amazing generosity, patience and talents of Richard Haywood, without whom much of my work – especially the artwork and technical stuff – would never have happened.

Thanks to my beautiful daughter Claire and wonderful son Daniel, to their extended family and my gorgeous grandchildren, my sister Stella, Sophie and Libby and all the other members of my family who don't really understand what it is I do, but try to support me enthusiastically anyway!